Grammar 4 Teacher's Book

Teaching grammar, spelling and punctuation with the
Grammar 4 Pupil Book

Written by

Sara Wernham and Sue Lloyd

Edited by Philippa Neville

Contents

PART 1

Introduction

For ease of use, this *Teacher's Book* has been divided into two distinct parts. The first part gives a comprehensive introduction, which explains the teaching method in detail. It is a good idea to read this part of the *Teacher's Book* before using the *Grammar 4 Pupil and Teacher's Books* in the classroom. The second part of the *Teacher's Book* provides a thorough and structured lesson plan for each day of teaching. The lesson plans in this part of the book are designed specifically for use with the corresponding pages in the *Grammar 4 Pupil Book*.

The *Grammar 4 Pupil and Teacher's Books* are designed to follow on from the *Grammar 1, 2* and *3 Pupil and Teacher's Books*. They are intended to:

- extend and refine the children's understanding of the grammar already taught,
- introduce new elements of grammar,
- teach new spelling patterns systematically,
- develop dictionary and thesaurus skills,
- improve vocabulary and comprehension, and
- reinforce the teaching in the *Grammar 1, 2* and *3 Pupil and Teacher's Books*.

Like the activities in the previous *Pupil Books*, the teaching in the *Grammar 4 Pupil Book* is multisensory and active. In the *Grammar 4 Pupil Book*, particular emphasis is placed on consolidating the children's learning and helping them to apply their new skills. As before in the *Grammar 1, 2* and *3 Pupil Books*, each part of speech is taught with an accompanying action and colour. The actions not only enliven the teaching, but also make the parts of speech easier for the children to remember. The colours, which are useful when identifying and labelling parts of speech in sentences, are the same as those used in Montessori Schools. As in previous *Teacher's Books*, the *Grammar 4 Teacher's Book* explains all the essential teaching ideas.

Children's Achievement

The most dramatic improvements to result from using the *Grammar 4 Pupil and Teacher's Books* will be found in the children's writing. After completing the *Grammar 4 Pupil Book*, the children will spell and punctuate more accurately, use a wider vocabulary and have a clearer understanding of how language works.

In their first year at school, the *Phonics Pupil Books* taught the children to write independently by listening for the sounds in words and choosing letters to represent those sounds. This enables the children to write pages of news and stories. It is a joy to read their work and to see the great pride and confidence they derive from their newly acquired skills. It is important to build on this foundation in the following years.

The *Grammar Pupil and Teacher's Books* provide teaching ideas designed to develop the children's writing skills. The children become more aware that they are writing for a purpose: that their words are intended to be read and understood. They learn that their writing is easier to understand if it is grammatically correct, accurately spelt, well punctuated and neatly written. The children also learn that, if they use interesting words, their writing can give real pleasure. Even in the early stages, it is valuable for the children to have a simple understanding of this long-term goal.

The Format of the Pupil and Teacher's Books

The programme for *Grammar 4* consists of a *Teacher's Book*, offering detailed lesson plans, and a corresponding *Pupil Book*, with activities for each lesson. Enough material is provided in these books for 36 weeks' teaching, with two lessons for each week. The *Grammar 4 Pupil Book* is designed so that there is one activity page for each lesson. Each lesson is intended to take up about one hour's teaching time.

Although it is referred to as the *Jolly Phonics* grammar programme, there are in fact two elements, namely spelling and grammar. The material in the *Pupil and Teacher's Books* is organised so that the first of the week's lessons concentrates on spelling and the second on grammar. However, the terms are used loosely and there is some overlap: punctuation and vocabulary development are among the areas covered in both spelling and grammar lessons. This is deliberate, as the two elements complement each other when combined.

The *Grammar 4* programme covers the more structured aspects of literacy, and is intended to take up only part of the teaching time set aside for literacy work. If two days' literacy lessons are devoted to *Grammar 4* each week, this leaves three lessons that can be devoted to the areas not covered by *Grammar 4*, such as comprehension, group and individual reading, formal and creative writing and handwriting practice. The children should be shown how spelling and grammar relate to their other literacy work. For instance, if the children have recently learnt about alliteration or onomatopoeia, and there are examples in the text they are studying, they can be encouraged to look at them and discuss the effects such language has on writing.

For each activity page in the *Pupil Book* there is a corresponding page in the *Teacher's Book*, offering a detailed lesson plan and useful teaching guidance. More detailed explanations and advice are provided in the two following sections: *Teaching Ideas for Grammar* and *Teaching Ideas for Spelling*. Relevant material from the *Grammar 1, 2* and *3 Teacher's Books* has also been included for easy reference.

To avoid confusion, the *Jolly Phonics* grammar materials follow the convention of using different parentheses to distinguish between letter names and letter sounds. Letter names are shown between these parentheses: ‹ ›. For example, the word *ship* begins with the letter ‹s›. By contrast, letter sounds are shown between these parentheses: / /. For example, the word *ship* begins with the /sh/ sound.

Teaching Ideas for Grammar

The benefits of learning grammar are cumulative. In the early stages, the children's grammar knowledge will help them to improve the clarity and quality of their writing. Later on, their grammar knowledge will help them to understand more complicated texts, learn foreign languages with greater ease, and use Standard English in their speech and writing.

The accents and dialects in spoken English vary from region to region. The grammar we learn first is picked up through our speech and varies accordingly. However, at times, there is a need for uniformity. If we all follow the same linguistic conventions, communication throughout the English-speaking world is greatly improved. An awareness of this fact helps those children who do not speak Standard English to understand that the way they speak is not wrong, but that it has not been chosen as the standard for the whole country. All children need to learn the standard form of English, as well as appreciating their own dialect.

In their first three years of *Grammar*, the children were introduced to the concepts of sentences, punctuation and parts of speech. In the *Grammar 1 Pupil Book*, they learnt about proper and common nouns, pronouns, verbs, adjectives and adverbs, and they learnt to use verbs to indicate whether something happened in the past, present or future. In the *Grammar 2 Pupil Book*, the children's knowledge was extended and their understanding deepened. Their knowledge of sentences was refined and they learnt to punctuate with greater variety and precision. They were also introduced to irregular verbs and to new parts of speech, namely possessive adjectives, conjunctions, prepositions and comparative and superlative adjectives. In the *Grammar 3 Pupil Book*, the children's understanding is further refined. They learnt how to distinguish between a phrase and a sentence, how to identify the subject and object of a sentence and how to organise sentences into paragraphs. In dictation, they received regular practice in writing direct speech with the proper punctuation. The children also learnt how to form the continuous tenses and were introduced to new parts of speech, namely collective nouns, irregular plurals, possessive pronouns and object pronouns. They also had regular dictionary and parsing practice with the aim of building their dictionary skills, improving their vocabulary and reinforcing their grammar knowledge.

The *Grammar 4 Pupil Book* extends, consolidates and refines the teaching of previous years. The children learn the difference between simple and compound sentences, about how statements can be turned into questions and how to distinguish between a phrase, a clause and an independent clause. They have regular parsing practice, both at sentence and verb level, to secure their understanding of parts of speech and of grammatical person and tense. The children are also introduced to the idea of simple subject-verb agreement, seeing what happens to the words in a sentence when a singular subject is made plural or, for example, when a sentence in the first person singular is rewritten in the third person. They are taught new parts of speech, namely infinitives and concrete, abstract and possessive nouns, and they continue to work on improving their vocabulary and writing, with a focus on developing their knowledge of homophones, antonyms, prefixes and suffixes, different forms of comparatives and superlatives, and learning new concepts like synonyms, noun phrases and onomatopoeia.

The *Grammar 4 Pupil Book* builds upon the teaching in the *Grammar 1, 2* and *3 Pupil Books*, so the children's understanding of this teaching must be secure before moving on. For this reason, it is important to go over anything the children are unsure of before introducing new concepts. The *Grammar Pupil Books* provide a systematic approach to revision. This enables even the slowest learners to keep up, while ensuring that more able children master their skills thoroughly and develop good grammatical habits. Every lesson should include some revision. Suggestions are provided in the lesson plans, but teachers should feel free to use their own judgment when deciding which areas their children need to revisit.

The term *grammar* is used broadly with children of this age. Definitions of the parts of speech, and of what constitutes a sentence, phrase and clause, have necessarily been simplified to age-appropriate working definitions. As the children grow older, these definitions can be expanded and refined.

Nouns

A noun denotes a person, place or thing. On the most basic level, nouns can be divided into proper nouns and common nouns.

Proper Nouns

Proper nouns were introduced in the *Grammar 1 Pupil Book* and revised in the subsequent levels. A proper noun starts with a capital letter, and is the particular name given to the following:

Action: The action for a **proper noun** is to touch one's forehead with the index and middle fingers. This is the same action as that used for *name* in British Sign Language.
Colour: The colour for all types of noun is black.

- a person, including that person's surname and title,
- a place, for example a river, mountain, park, street, town, country, continent or planet,
- a building, for example a school, house, library, swimming pool or cinema,
- a date, for example a day of the week, a month or a religious holiday.

In the *Grammar 1 Pupil Book* the main focus was on people's names being proper nouns. In the *Grammar 2 Pupil Book* the names of the months, including their correct spelling and sequence, were the focus. In the *Grammar 3 Pupil Book* the focus moved to place names. The children learnt that in longer place names, such as the *Tower of London*, only the important words need a capital letter, not the short joining words.

Common Nouns

All nouns that are not specific names or titles are called common nouns. Common nouns can be further divided into concrete nouns (e.g. *table* or *child*), abstract nouns (e.g. *warmth* or *kindness*), and collective nouns (e.g. *the **group*** or *a **flock** of birds*). Although there are three types of common noun, only concrete nouns are taught in the early stages. The intangible nature of abstract nouns, like *happiness*, means that they are difficult for young children to grasp.

Action: The action for a **common noun** is to touch one's forehead with all the fingers of one hand.
Colour: The colour for all types of noun is black.

Everything we can see has a name by which we can refer to it: for example, *table*, *chair* and *pencil*. As these names are not specific to any one object, but refer to tables, chairs and so on in general, they are called common nouns and not proper nouns. At this stage the children find it useful to think of nouns as the names for things they can see and touch. A good way to help the children decide if a word is a noun is to encourage them to say *a, an* or *the* before the word and see whether it makes sense. For example, *a chair, an elephant* and *the table* make sense, whereas *a fell, an unhappy* and *the ran* do not. (The words *a, an* and *the* are the three articles, and are explained later.)

In general, children understand the concept of nouns easily and have no trouble when asked to think of examples. Despite this, it can still be difficult for them to identify nouns in written sentences. This becomes easier with regular parsing practice, which is provided at the bottom of the spelling pages.

Collective Nouns

Collective nouns were introduced in the *Grammar 3 Pupil Book*; they are words used to describe groups of people, animals or things: for example, *a **crowd** of people, a **herd** of cows* or *a **fleet** of ships*. Collective nouns can also describe groups of abstract nouns: for example, *a **host** of ideas* or *a **wash** of emotions*. Abstract nouns are explained below.

Collective nouns are usually singular (e.g. *a bunch, a band, a flock*) because they describe the group as a whole; whereas the nouns that make up the group are plural (e.g. *a bunch of **flowers**, a band of **robbers**, a flock of **birds***) because there are many of them. Collective nouns are a type of common noun, so they do not need a capital letter. Often, the same collective noun can be used to describe a number of different things; for example, *bunch* can be used to describe, among other things, flowers, keys and bananas. Sometimes more than one collective noun can be used to describe the same item; for example, a group of whales can be described as *a pod* or *a school*. Many collective nouns are used to describe groups of animals and birds. Some are very common (e.g. *herd, flock, pride*), while others, particularly those used for birds, are quite obscure (e.g. *a **murder** of crows*). Many new collective nouns, like *a **bounce** of kangaroos*, are not officially recognised, but are nevertheless entertaining for the children.

It is important not to confuse collective nouns with uncountable nouns. Uncountable nouns, such as *furniture, water* and *meat*, are almost always singular. Collective nouns, on the other hand, can be referred to in the plural when they describe more than one group of a particular type of object (e.g. *two **colonies** of ants*).

Concrete Nouns

In the *Grammar 4 Pupil Book*, the children learn that the things they can see, hear, smell, taste or touch – that is, things that exist in a physical form – are called concrete nouns. The children are encouraged to think about different types of concrete noun and to categorise them according to the five senses.

Action: The action for a **concrete noun** is to gently tap one's forehead twice with one hand.
Colour: The colour for all types of noun is black.

Abstract Nouns

Once the children have learnt about concrete nouns, they can be introduced to the concept of abstract nouns. In the *Grammar 4 Pupil Book*, the children learn that abstract nouns are things that cannot be experienced through the five senses. They are typically the names for things like ideas (e.g. *justice*

Action: The action for an **abstract noun** is to move one's hand away from the forehead in a spiral action.
Colour: The colour for all types of noun is black.

or *peace*), feelings (e.g. *anger* or *love*), qualities (e.g. *bravery* or *wisdom*), and actions and events (e.g. *a walk* or *a meeting*). Children should be at the stage now where they are able to understand the concept of abstract nouns, at least in principle. With regular parsing practice they will find it easier to identify abstract nouns in their reading and writing.

Possessive Nouns

In the *Grammar 2 Pupil Book*, the children were taught that adding ‹'s› to a person's name shows possession, so that *Tiffany's bike* means *the bike belonging to Tiffany*. The apostrophe is there to show that the ‹s› is not there to make the proper noun plural. In the *Grammar 4 Pupil Book*, the children go on to learn that this is called a possessive noun. They learn that common nouns, as well as proper nouns, can be possessive, as in *the **girl's** coat* and *the **kangaroo's** pouch*. The children are also taught that possessive nouns can be plural. Most plurals already end in ‹s›, in which case only the apostrophe is required, as in *the **girls'** coats* and *the **kangaroos'** pouches*. However, if the plural is irregular and does not end in ‹s›, both the apostrophe and the ‹s› are added, as in *the **men's** watches* or *some **mice's** tails*.

It is important the children do not confuse *it's*, which is a contraction of *it is*, with the possessive adjective *its*. Possessive adjectives (covered in more detail on pages 11 to 12) are used in place of possessive nouns, so that *the **girl's** coat* becomes **her** *coat* and *the **kangaroo's** pouch* becomes **its** *pouch*. Possessive adjectives already indicate possession so they do not need an apostrophe ‹s›. With regular practice, the children will learn to distinguish between the homophones *it's* and *its* and use them correctly in their writing.

Despite its name, a possessive noun acts as an adjective in a sentence because it describes another noun. The children are already familiar with the idea that nouns can function as adjectives; in the *Grammar 3 Pupil Book* they learnt that nouns act as adjectives in compound words such as **apple** *pie* and **rabbit** *hutch*.

Plurals

Most nouns change in the plural, that is, when they describe more than one. In the early *Grammar Pupil Books,* the two main ways of forming the plural were introduced: adding ‹-s› to the noun (as in *dogs* and *boys*), and adding ‹-es› to those nouns that end with ‹sh›, ‹ch›, ‹s›, ‹z› or ‹x› (as in *brushes, dresses* and *foxes*). These endings often sound like /z/ and /iz/, respectively, as in *girls* and *boxes*. Learning that these words are plurals will help the children remember to spell the /z/ sound correctly. In the *Grammar 3 Pupil Book*, the children learnt that nouns ending in ‹o› also take the ‹-es› suffix, unless the word is foreign, abbreviated, or has a vowel before the ‹o›, as in *pianos, kilos* and *studios*.

In the *Grammar 2 Pupil Book*, the children also learnt the two ways of forming the plural of nouns that end with a ‹y›. If the letter immediately before the ‹y› is a vowel, then the plural is simply made in the usual way by adding ‹-s› (as in *days, boys* and *monkeys*). However, if the letter immediately before the ‹y› is a consonant, then ‹y› is replaced by a 'shy ‹i›' before adding ‹-es› (as in *flies, babies* and *puppies*). The children should already know that 'shy ‹i›' does not like to be at the end of a word and is often replaced by 'toughy ‹y›'. This helps them understand that while we would be unlikely to find 'shy ‹i›' at the end of a word like *puppy*, we will find it in the plural, *puppies*, when 'shy ‹i›' is no longer at the end of the word.

The *Grammar 2 Pupil Book* also introduced some common irregular, or 'tricky', plurals in the weekly spelling lists (e.g. *children* from *child, women* from *woman,* and *mice* from *mouse*). Tricky plurals can be formed by modifying the root word, altering its pronunciation, adding an unusual ending, or a combination of the three. Sometimes, the pronunciation of the root word alters even when the spelling does not; for instance, the letter ‹i› makes a long /ie/ sound in *child*, but a short /i/ sound in *children*. Some plurals, such as *sheep, fish* and *deer*, are tricky because they have the same form for both singular and plural.

In the *Grammar 4 Pupil Book*, the children learn that other plurals are tricky because their singular forms end in ‹f› or ‹fe›, whereas their plurals are made by removing the ending and adding ‹-ves›, as in *shelves* and *knives*. Not all singular nouns ending in ‹f› or ‹fe› make their plurals in this way, so the spellings have to be learnt. The children also learn that, when using a plural in a sentence, the other words connected to it must agree. While most children will be making these adjustments automatically, the teaching is made more explicit in the *Grammar 4 Pupil Book* (see page 17, Grammatical Agreement).

Pronouns

Pronouns are the little words used to replace nouns. Without them, language would become boring and repetitive. They can be divided into personal pronouns (e.g. *I* and *me*), possessive pronouns (e.g. *mine*), relative pronouns (e.g. *who*) and reflexive pronouns (e.g. *myself*). Only personal pronouns were taught in the early *Grammar Pupil Books*. Possessive pronouns were introduced in the *Grammar 3 Pupil Book*. The relative pronouns and reflexive pronouns can be taught when the children are older.

Personal Pronouns

In the *Grammar 1 Pupil Book*, the children were taught the eight personal pronouns: *I, you, he, she, it, we, you* and *they*. In modern English, we use the same word, *you*, for both the second person singular

Singular Pronoun Actions:

I (me): point to oneself
you (you): point to someone else
he (him): point to a boy
she (her): point to a girl
it (it): point to the floor

Plural Pronoun Actions:

we (us): point in a circle including oneself and others
you (you): point to two other people
they (them): point to the next-door class

Colour: The colour for pronouns is pink.

pronoun and the second person plural pronoun, but this is not the case in many foreign languages. In order to make learning such languages easier later on, the *Grammar Pupil Books* introduce the children to the distinction between *you* used in the singular and *you* used in the plural.

In the *Grammar 3 Pupil Book*, the children learnt how to identify the subject and the object of a sentence. They also learnt that the personal pronouns can change, depending on whether they are the subject or the object of the sentence. In the *Grammar 4 Pupil Book*, the children learn that personal pronouns are called 'personal' because they mostly relate to people: when talking about ourselves, we use *I* and *we*; when talking directly to one or more people, we say *you*; and when talking about someone or something else, we use *he*, *she* and *it* for the singular and *they* for the plural. These three groups are known as first, second and third person and they can be singular or plural (see below). Once the children are introduced to grammatical person, they are given regular practice parsing the verb in the spelling lessons. They also learn that when the person in a sentence is changed, the verb and the rest of the sentence must agree.

Subject Pronouns	I	you	he	she	it	we	you	they
Object Pronouns	me	you	him	her	it	us	you	them

The children practise using the subject pronouns whenever they conjugate verbs. They do the actions and say, for example, *I swim, you swim, he swims, she swims, it swims, we swim, you swim, they swim*. These same actions can also be used to revise the object pronouns.

Possessive Pronouns

There are eight possessive pronouns: *mine, yours, his, hers, its, ours, yours* and *theirs*. These pronouns correspond to the personal pronouns: *I/me, you/you, he/him, she/her, it/it, we/us, you/you, they/them*, and the possessive adjectives: *my, your, his, her, its, our, your, their*. Possessive pronouns replace a noun and its possessive adjective, so that *my hat* becomes *mine*, and *their house* becomes *theirs*. These pronouns are possessive because they indicate who the noun (which they are also replacing) belongs to. Possessive pronouns can be practised using the same colour and actions as for the personal pronouns.

Verbs

A verb denotes what a person or thing does or is. It can describe an action, an event, a state or a change. It is easiest for children to think of verbs as 'doing words' at first. The infinitive form of a verb is made by putting the word *to* before the verb root, as in *to run,*

Action: The action for **verbs** in general is to clench fists and move arms backwards and forwards at one's sides, as if running.
Colour: The colour for all types of verb is red.

to hop, to sing and *to play*. Early on the children learn that an infinitive is the 'name' of the verb, but gradually the term *infinitive* should be introduced. In the *Grammar 4 Pupil Book* the children learn that infinitives can be used in a sentence, although they are never the main verb and do not have a subject.

The children were introduced to verbs in the *Grammar 1 Pupil Book*, where they learnt to conjugate regular verbs in the present, past and future (because verbs in English are very complicated, only the simple tenses were introduced initially). Conjugating means choosing a particular verb and saying the pronouns in order with the correct form of the verb after each one. Conjugating verbs aloud with the pronoun actions is very good practice for children. It promotes a strong understanding of how verbs work, which helps them make sense of their own language, and is invaluable when they come to learn foreign languages later on. Revise the conjugations regularly, using the pronoun actions.

Past	*I jumped*	*you jumped*	*he jumped*	*she jumped*	*it jumped*
	we jumped	*you jumped*		*they jumped*	
Present	*I jump*	*you jump*	*he jumps*	*she jumps*	*it jumps*
	we jump	*you jump*		*they jump*	
Future	*I shall / will jump*	*you will jump*	*he will jump*	*she will jump*	*it will jump*
	we shall / will jump	*you will jump*		*they will jump*	

The children need to remember the following points:
- In the simple present tense, the verb changes after the third person singular pronouns: *he, she* and *it*. For regular verbs, ‹-s› is added to the root (except when the word ends in ‹sh›, ‹ch›, ‹s›, ‹z›, or ‹x›, when ‹-es› is added). This is called the third person singular marker.
- The simple past tense of regular verbs is formed by adding the suffix ‹-ed› to the root. If the root ends in ‹e› (as in *bake*), the final ‹e› must be removed before ‹-ed› is added. The ‹-ed› can be pronounced in one of three ways: /t/ (as in *slipped*), /d/ (as in *smiled*) or /id/ (as in *waited*).
- With simple verbs, we add the auxiliary verbs *shall* or *will* to the verb root to denote the future. The auxiliary verb *will* can be used with all of the pronouns, but *shall* should only be used with *I* or *we*.

The children learnt these regular conjugations in the *Grammar 1* and *Grammar 2 Pupil Books*, and continued to revise them in the *Grammar 3 Pupil Book*. In the *Grammar 2 Pupil Book*, the children were also introduced to some of the most common irregular, or 'tricky', verbs and their past forms: for example, *sat* (from *to sit*), and *ran* (from *to run*). In addition, they learnt to conjugate and identify the irregular verb *to be* in both the present and past tenses. This is especially useful for those children who are not in the habit of using standard forms in their speech: children who say, for example, *we was* instead of *we were*. Chanting the conjugations regularly will help these children avoid making mistakes in their written work.

The irregularity of the verb *to be* often makes it difficult for the children to identify in sentences. It is important to overcome this problem, as the verb *to be* is used frequently. In the *Grammar 2 Pupil Book*, the children learnt that every sentence must contain a verb and they were taught to identify sentences by looking for the verb. For this reason, it is crucial that the children are able to identify all verbs with confidence.

A familiarity with the verb *to be* also helped the children when they came to learn the continuous tenses in the *Grammar 3 Pupil Book*. The continuous tenses (e.g. *I am walking, I was walking, I shall be walking*) are formed by adding the present participle (e.g. *walking*) to the auxiliary verb *to be*. In order to form the continuous future, the children must first learn the future of the verb *to be*, which was introduced early on in the *Grammar 3 Pupil Book*. Once the children have learnt how to form the continuous tenses, it is important to give them plenty of practice in identifying all of the verb tenses taught so far. In this way, they will be able to distinguish between the simple and continuous forms more easily and this in turn will help them understand how the different tenses are used.

For now, it is enough that the children understand that the simple present is used to describe an action that is repeated or usual (such as, *I swim in the pool every day*), and the present continuous is used to describe something that has started, is continuing, and has not stopped yet: either an action happening right now (e.g. *I am swimming in the pool*), or a longer action in progress, but one which is not necessarily happening at this moment (e.g. *I am learning to swim*). The simple past and simple future describe actions that have started and finished, or will start and finish, within a specific time (such as, *I swam in the pool today*, and *I shall swim in the pool later*), while the past and future continuous describe an ongoing action.

There are other uses of these tenses, but they can be taught along with the perfect tenses when the children are older. For reference, the table below shows all three forms in past, present and future.

	Past	Present	Future
Simple	*looked*	*look*	*will look*
Continuous	*was looking*	*is looking*	*will be looking*
Perfect	*had looked*	*have looked*	*will have looked*

In the *Grammar 2 Pupil Book*, the children were taught how to add the ‹-ing› suffix to verb roots. In the *Grammar 3 Pupil Book*, the children learnt that this form of the verb is called the present participle. In the *Grammar 4 Pupil Book*, the children learn that the present participle can be used as an adjective, (e.g. *There was no running water*), and later they can learn that the present participle is also used to make the gerund form (the noun form) of a verb (e.g. *I like running*).

Technically there is no future tense in English since, unlike the past tense, the future is not formed by modifying the verb root itself. However, at this stage it is helpful for the children to think of verbs as taking place in the past, present or future. The complexities can be taught when the children are older.

Past Tense Action: The **past tense** action is pointing backwards over one's shoulder with a thumb.

Present Tense Action: The **present tense** action is pointing towards the floor with the palm of the hand.

Future Action: The action for verbs that describe the **future** is pointing towards the front.

Adjectives

An adjective is a word that describes a noun or pronoun. It can be used either directly before the noun or pronoun, as in *the **big** dog*, or elsewhere in the sentence, as in *the dog was **big***. The children are encouraged to use adjectives imaginatively in their writing.

Action: The action for all types of **adjective**, including **possessive adjectives**, and **comparatives** and **superlatives**, is to touch the side of the temple with one's fist.
Colour: The colour for all types of adjective is blue.

Adjectives were introduced in the *Grammar 1 Pupil Book*, where the children learnt how to use them before a noun. In the *Grammar 2 Pupil Book*, adjectives were revised, and the children practised identifying them wherever they were placed in the sentence. In the *Grammar 3* and *4 Pupil Books*, the children learn that adjectives can sometimes be formed by adding certain suffixes to other words: for example, by adding the suffixes ‹-y› or ‹-al› to a noun, as in *windy* and *logical*, or by adding suffixes like ‹-less›, ‹-ful› and ‹-able›, as in *helpless, helpful* and *enjoyable*. The children also learn that other parts of speech can sometimes act as adjectives: for example, in the compound word *apple pie*, the first noun *apple* is describing the main noun *pie*; in the phrase *the running water*, the present participle *running*, which is a verb form, is describing the water; and possessive nouns always act as adjectives to describe another noun, as in the *peacock's tail*.

Possessive Adjectives

The children's understanding of adjectives was extended in the *Grammar 2 Pupil Book* to include the eight possessive adjectives: *my, your, his, her, its, our, your* and *their*. These correspond to the personal pronouns: *I/me, you/you, he/him, she/her, it/it, we/us, you/you, they/them*, and the possessive pronouns: *mine, yours, his, hers, its, ours, yours, theirs*. A possessive adjective replaces one noun and describes another, by saying whose it is. For example, in the sentence *Lucy fed her cat*, the possessive adjective *her* is used in place of *Lucy's* and describes *cat*, by saying whose cat it is. (As the possessive adjectives also function as pronouns, they are sometimes known as the 'weak' set of possessive pronouns. However, to avoid any confusion with the 'strong' set of possessive pronouns, like *mine*, the *Grammar Pupil and Teacher's Books* do not use this terminology.)

Comparatives and Superlatives

The adjectives introduced in the *Grammar 1 Pupil Book* are called positive adjectives; they describe a noun or a pronoun without comparing it to anything else (as in *the girl is **young***). In the *Grammar 2 Pupil Book*, comparative and superlative adjectives were introduced. These adjectives describe a noun or a pronoun by comparing it to other items. A comparative is used when comparing a noun to one or more other items (as in *this boy is **younger** than Jim and Ted*). A superlative is used when comparing a noun to the other items in a group to which that noun also belongs (as in *he is the **youngest** boy on the team*).

Short positive adjectives usually form their comparatives and superlatives with the suffixes ‹-er› and ‹-est›: for example, *hard, harder, hardest*. In the *Grammar 4 Pupil Book*, the children learn that with longer adjectives, we often use the words *more* and *most*: for example, *difficult, more difficult, most difficult*. However, some two-syllable adjectives also make their comparative and superlative by adding *more* and *most*, especially those which have a suffix, as in *most careful, more helpless, most daring, more shaded* and *most famous*. The children need to listen and decide which sounds right in the sentence. The children also learn about other comparative and superlative forms, such as *less* and *least*, *better* and *best*, *worse* and *worst*.

Adverbs

An adverb is similar to an adjective, in that they are both describing words. However, an adverb describes a verb rather than a noun. Usually, adverbs describe how, where, when or how often something happens. Adverbs can also be used to modify adjectives or other adverbs, but the children do not need to know that at this stage.

Action: The action for an **adverb** is to bang one fist on top of the other.
Colour: The colour for adverbs is orange.

The children were introduced to adverbs in the *Grammar 1 Pupil Book*. Initially, they were taught to think of an adverb as a word often ending with the suffix ‹-ly›. In the *Grammar 2 Pupil Book*, adverbs were revised and the children were encouraged to identify less obvious adverbs by looking at the verb and deciding which word describes it. For example, in the sentence, *We arrived late last night*, the adverb *late* tells us something about the past tense verb *arrived*. Point out examples of adverbs in text whenever possible to help the children develop this understanding. In the *Grammar 3 Pupil Book*, the children learnt that adjectives can sometimes be turned into adverbs by adding the suffix ‹-ly›, as in *quickly, slowly* and *softly*. In the *Grammar 4 Pupil Book*, the children learn that adjectives can be turned into adverbs by adding ‹-ly› or ‹-ally› when the adjective ends in ‹-ical› or ‹-ic›, as in *musically* and *basically*.

Prepositions

A preposition is a word that relates one noun or pronoun to another. In the sentence, *He climbed over the gate*, for example, the preposition *over* relates *he* to *gate*. The 'pre' of preposition means *before* and 'position'

Action: The action for **prepositions** is to point from one noun to another.
Colour: The colour for prepositions is green.

means *place*, so together preposition means *placed before*, because it is placed before a noun or pronoun. A preposition is also placed before any describing words that may already come before the noun or pronoun (words such as adjectives, possessive adjectives or the articles *a, an* and *the*), as in the phrases ***after** a long pause, **by** her favourite author, **in** my purse, **under** the bridge*.

Prepositions, as introduced in the *Grammar 2 Pupil Book*, often describe where something is or what it is moving towards. Practise prepositions by calling out examples and asking for nouns to go with them. For example, for *in*, the children might suggest *the box* or *the classroom*, and for *under* they might suggest *the mat* or *the table*. Many common prepositions are short words like *at, by, for, of, in, on, to* and *up*. Other common examples include: *above, after, around, behind, beside, between, down, from, into, past, through, towards, under* and *with*. However, many of these words can also function as adverbs if they do not come before a noun or pronoun. For example, in the sentence, *I fell down*, the word *down* is an adverb that describes *fell*, whereas in *I fell down the stairs*, the word *down* is a preposition that relates *I* to *stairs*.

Conjunctions

A conjunction is a word used to join parts of a sentence that usually, but not always, contain their own verbs. Conjunctions allow the children to write longer, less repetitive sentences. Instead of writing, for example, *I eat fish. I eat peas. I like the taste*, the children could use the conjunctions *and* and *because* to write: *I eat fish and peas because I like the taste*. Where the shorter sentences were stilted and repetitive, the new one is flowing and concise.

Action: The action for **conjunctions** is to hold one's hands apart with palms facing up. Move both hands so one is on top of the other.
Colour: The colour for conjunctions is purple.

The *Grammar 2 Pupil Book* introduced conjunctions, focusing on six of the most useful ones: *and, but, because, or, so,* and *while*. In the *Grammar 4 Pupil Book*, the children learn that the conjunctions *for, and, nor, but, or, yet* and *so* can be used to join two simple sentences to make a compound sentence. When the children are older they will learn that these are called the co-ordinating conjunctions and can be remembered by the acronym FANBOYS.

The ability to vary the length of their sentences will greatly improve the quality of the children's writing. Display a list of common conjunctions in the classroom to encourage the children to use other words besides *and*: examples include *although, if, now, once, since, unless, until, when* and *whether*.

Definite and Indefinite Articles: the, a, an

The words *a, an* and *the* are known as articles. *A* and *an* are used before singular nouns and are called the indefinite articles, as in *a man* and *an egg*. *The* is used before singular and plural nouns and is called the definite article, as in *the dog* and *the boys*. The articles are a special sort of adjective, although the term *determiner* is often used as well. Determiners are words used in front of nouns to show, or determine, which things or people are being referred to.

In the *Grammar 1 Pupil Book*, the children learnt when to use *an* instead of *a*. They were taught to choose the correct article by looking at the noun that follows it. When the noun begins with a vowel sound, the correct article is *an*, as in *an ant, an eagle, an igloo, an octopus, an umpire*. Otherwise, the correct article is *a*. Note that it is the first sound that is important, not necessarily the first letter. If, for example, a word starts with a silent consonant and the first sound is actually a vowel, the correct article is *an*, as in *an hour*. If, on the other hand, the word starts with the long vowel /ue/, pronounced /y-oo/, then the correct article is *a*, as in *a unicorn*.

Simple and Compound Sentences

The full definition of a sentence is complicated and so, in the *Grammar Pupil Books*, a simple working definition is gradually expanded and refined: in the *Grammar 1 Pupil Book*, the children learnt that a sentence must start with a capital letter, end with a full stop, and make sense. In the *Grammar 2 Pupil Book*, the children learnt that a sentence must always have a verb and end with a full stop, question mark or exclamation mark. In the *Grammar 3 Pupil Book*, this definition was further refined when the children learnt that a sentence always has a subject and may have an object; the subject is the noun or pronoun that 'does' the verb action, as in **Sam** *hit the ball* and the object is the noun or pronoun that 'receives' the verb action, as in *The ball hit* **Sam**. In the *Grammar 4 Pupil Book*, the children learn that when two or more sentences are joined together with one of the co-ordinating conjunctions (*for*, *and*, *nor*, *but*, *or*, *yet* and *so*), it is called a compound sentence, and the two original sentences are called simple sentences.

Statements, Questions and Exclamations

In the *Grammar 1* and *2 Pupil Books*, the children learnt to recognise a question as a sentence that asks for further information and ends in a question mark. They were also taught the ‹wh› question words (*what*, *why*, *when*, *where*, *who*, *which*, *whose*). In the *Grammar 2 Pupil Book*, the children's knowledge was extended as they were introduced to exclamation marks, which are used at the end of exclamations to show that the writer or speaker feels strongly about something. Later, in the *Grammar 3 Pupil Book*, they learnt how to write questions and exclamations in direct speech.

In the *Grammar 4 Pupil Book*, the children learn that sentences ending in a full stop are called statements, and they look at some simple ways to turn statements into questions. If the main verb in a statement is *to be*, as in *This **is** the way to the park*, it can be made into a question simply by moving the verb to the beginning of the sentence and replacing the full stop with a question mark: **Is** *this the way to the park?* If the sentence has a main verb and an auxiliary, as in *I **can go** to the park*, only the auxiliary verb is moved to the front: **Can** *I **go** to the park?* Later, the children can learn that statements written in the simple past and simple present cannot be turned into questions in this way because they have no auxiliary verb. Instead the auxiliary *do/does* (simple present) and *did* (simple past) is added at the beginning of the sentence, so that *You went to the park* becomes **Did** *you go to the park?* using the infinitive form for the main verb.

Phrases

A phrase is a group of words that makes sense but has no verb and subject. In the *Grammar 3 Pupil Book*, the children learnt to distinguish between a sentence and a phrase. Now, in the *Grammar 4 Pupil Book*, the children learn that a noun, together with the words that describe (or modify) it, is called a noun phrase. There can be more than one noun phrase in a sentence and each noun phrase can be replaced with a pronoun. For example, in the sentence *I took three juicy apples from the big wooden bowl*, there are two noun phrases: *three juicy apples* and *the big wooden bowl*. These can be replaced by the pronouns *them* and *it* and still make grammatical sense: *I took them from it*. Not all words in a noun phrase come before the noun, as in *a girl with blonde hair*. This kind of noun phrase generally has a main noun (*girl*) and another noun helping to describe it (*hair*).

Clauses

The *Grammar 4 Pupil Book* also introduces clauses. A clause is a group of words that contains a subject and verb and makes sense. This is much like the working definition of a sentence; indeed, some clauses, called independent clauses, can stand alone as sentences, such as those found in a compound sentence. However, not all clauses are independent. For example, in the sentence *While he waited, he read his book*, the clause *he read his book* could stand alone as a simple sentence. However, *While he waited* could not, as it is not a complete thought; although it has a subject, a verb and makes sense, it leaves us to ask what else the subject did during that time. This type of clause is called a dependent or subordinate clause. Later, the children can learn that a sentence with both an independent clause and a dependent clause is called a complex sentence.

Paragraphs

In the *Grammar 3 Pupil Book,* the children began to learn about paragraphs. Paragraphs are used to organise information in a piece of writing so that it is easy to read and understand. Instead of one large block of text, writing is broken down into smaller groups of sentences called paragraphs. Each paragraph starts on a new line and is made up of sentences that describe one idea or topic. By putting paragraphs in a particular order, a piece of writing can move from one idea to another in a way that makes sense.

The children are encouraged to think about what they want to say and organise their thoughts before they start writing. They learn how to break down the topic they want to write about into subtopics and place their different ideas under subheadings. This helps them to make their writing flow and be more interesting. The children should be encouraged to write in paragraphs from now on.

Punctuation

The *Grammar Pupil Books* emphasise the importance of punctuation. The children are taught that their writing will be easier to read if it is accurately punctuated. In the *Grammar 2 Pupil Book*, the children revised full stops, question marks and speech marks, and were introduced to exclamation marks, commas and apostrophes. In the *Grammar 3* and *4 Pupil Books*, the focus is on using the correct punctuation when writing direct speech. In direct speech, the words are written exactly as they are said: for example, *'I'm tired,' said Tim.* (This is different from reported speech: for example, *Tim said he was tired.*) The children also revise speech marks, full stops, commas and contractions, and learn how to use question marks and exclamation marks in direct speech.

Question Marks ‹?›

The children need to understand what a question is and how to form a question mark correctly. If a sentence is worded in such a way that it expects an answer, then it is a question and needs a question mark instead of a full stop. If the question is being written as direct speech, the question mark is kept at the end and not replaced with a comma.

Exclamation Marks ‹!›

An exclamation mark is used at the end of a sentence, instead of a full stop, to show that the speaker or writer feels strongly about something. When someone exclaims, they cry out suddenly, especially in anger, surprise or pain. What they say is called an exclamation. If the exclamation is being written as direct speech, the exclamation mark is kept at the end and not replaced with a comma.

Commas ‹,›

Sometimes it is necessary to indicate a short pause in the middle of a sentence, where it would be wrong to use a full stop. This helps the reader separate one idea from another. For this sort of pause we use a comma. The children will be used to being told to pause when they see a comma in their reading. However, learning when to use commas in writing is more difficult. The *Grammar 2 Pupil Book* introduced two of the most straightforward ways commas are used:
1. We use commas to separate items in a list of more than two items: *red, white and blue,* or *Grandma, Grandpa, Aunt and Uncle.* Note that a comma is not used before the last item in a list, but is replaced by the word *and* or *or.*
2. We also use commas in sentences that include direct speech. Here, the comma indicates a pause between the words spoken and the rest of the sentence. If the speech comes before the rest of the sentence, the comma belongs after the last word spoken but inside the speech marks: *I am hungry,' complained Matt.* (If the words spoken are a question or an exclamation, then a question mark or exclamation mark is used instead of a comma in the same position.) If the speech comes after the rest of the sentence, the comma belongs after the last word that is not spoken but before the speech marks: *Matt complained, 'I am hungry.'*

Apostrophes ‹'›

The *Grammar 2 Pupil Book* introduced both of the main ways that an apostrophe is used. Apostrophes are very often incorrectly used. There are clear rules for using apostrophes and it is important to teach them early on before any children develop bad habits in their writing.

- An apostrophe followed by the letter ‹s› is used after a noun to indicate possession, as in *Ben's new toy* or *the girl's father*. The apostrophe is needed to show that the ‹s› is not being used to make a plural. Understanding this distinction will help the children use apostrophe ‹s› correctly. Encourage the children to think about the meaning of what they write and decide whether each ‹s› is being used to make a plural or the possessive case.

    In the *Grammar 4 Pupil Book*, the children learn how to use apostrophe ‹s› with plurals that end in ‹s› (e.g. *the boys' room*). These are called possessive nouns. Later, the children can learn how to use apostrophe ‹s› with names that end in ‹es› (e.g. *James' cat*).

    Although the possessive adjectives (e.g. *my, your, his*) indicate possession, there is no risk of confusion with the plural, so they do not need an apostrophe. However, it is important to help the children avoid the common mistake of writing the possessive adjective *its* as *it's*.

- An apostrophe is also used to show that a letter (or more than one letter) is missing. Sometimes, we shorten a pair of words by joining them together and leaving out some of their letters. We use an apostrophe to show where the missing letter (or letters) used to be. This is called a contraction. There are many common contractions, such as *I'm* (I am), *didn't* (did not) and *you'll* (you will).

    Encourage the children to listen to each contraction and identify which sound or sounds are missing. This will help them to leave out the appropriate letters and put the apostrophe in the right place, thereby avoiding some common mistakes. In *haven't*, for example, the /o/ of *not* is missing, so the apostrophe goes between ‹n› and ‹t›, to show where ‹o› used to be. It does not go between ‹e› and ‹n›, as in 'have'nt'. When *it is* is contracted to *it's*, as in *it's late*, an apostrophe is needed to show that the second ‹i› is missing. The children need to think about the meaning of what they are writing, so as to avoid confusion with the possessive adjective *its*. It is important that the children learn how to spell and punctuate contractions correctly. However, they should only use contractions when writing direct speech or informal notes. Contractions are not traditionally used in formal writing.

Hyphens ‹-›

Sometimes it is necessary to show that two or more words, or parts of words, are linked closely together, either in use or meaning. This helps the reader understand the text properly and avoids ambiguity. To do this we use a hyphen. Hyphens are found mostly in compound words and some words with a prefix, especially when it makes a word easier to read, as in *brother-in-law*, or avoids confusion with another word, as in *re-cover*.

However, not all compound words or words with a prefix need a hyphen, and hyphens are not used so commonly now as they once were; whether a hyphen is used or not often changes over time, and varies between dictionaries. Also, the rules for when to use hyphens are quite complex for children of this age, and so they should be encouraged to check such words in a dictionary and then make sure they use the spelling consistently in their writing.

Nevertheless, there are some instances in which a hyphen is nearly always used and these, along with the term *hyphen*, are introduced in the *Grammar 4 Pupil Book*. The children learn to use a hyphen when the numbers between 21 and 99 are written as words, as in *twenty-one* or *thirty-three*, and when the first part of a compound word is a capital letter, as in *X-ray* and *T-shirt*. Later, children can learn about other common uses of the hyphen. These include joining fractions, as in *three-quarters* and *two-thirds*, and when a compound adjective comes directly before the noun it is describing, as in *the well-known phrase*. For now it is enough that the children understand what a hyphen is and how it can be used to make meaning clearer.

Parsing: identifying parts of speech in sentences

Parsing means identifying the function, or part of speech, of each word in a sentence. The children must look at each word in context to decide what part of speech it is. This skill is worth promoting, as it reinforces the grammar teaching and helps the children to develop an analytical understanding of how our language works. Many words can function as more than one part of speech. For example, the word *light* can be a noun (*the light*), a verb (*to light*), or an adjective (*a light colour*). It is only by analysing a word's use within a sentence that its function can be identified.

The best way to introduce parsing is by writing extremely simple sentences on the board. A good example is: *I pat the dog.* This can be parsed as: pronoun, verb, article, noun. Ask the children to identify the parts of speech they know (in this case: pronoun, verb, noun). They enjoy taking turns to underline the parts of speech in the appropriate colours. Gradually, when most of the children have mastered this, move on to more complicated sentences that use more parts of speech: for example, *She cheerfully wrote a long letter to her friend.* This can be parsed as: pronoun, adverb, verb (the infinitive of which is *to write*), (article,) adjective, noun, preposition, possessive adjective, noun. Remind the children that every sentence must contain at least one verb. They should begin parsing a sentence by identifying the verb (or verbs), and should supply each verb in the infinitive form. If there is time, the children should identify as many of the other parts of speech as possible, underlining them in the appropriate colours (as shown in the parsing colour key below).

Nouns	Verbs	Pronouns	Adjectives	Adverbs	Prepositions	Conjunctions
(Black)	(Red)	(Pink)	(Blue)	(Orange)	(Green)	(Purple)

In the *Grammar 3* and *4 Pupil Books*, the regular parsing practice in the spelling lessons will help the children become quick and competent at this task. If any children are unfamiliar with parsing, or find it difficult, they need to work on simpler sentences and build up their confidence.

Grammatical Agreement

From the beginning, the children are encouraged to think about the relationship between words in a sentence and to use their grammar knowledge to make their writing as clear and as accurate as possible. They learn that the indefinite articles *a* and *an* are only used with a singular noun, whereas the definite article *the* can be used for both singular and plural. They learn how to form a plural correctly and how to conjugate a verb. They also learn the personal pronouns and possessive adjectives and understand how they differ.

This knowledge helps children when they come to learn about grammatical agreement, which is introduced in the *Grammar 4 Pupil Book*. In most languages, certain word relationships have to match or agree. In English this agreement centres on person, number and sometimes gender. The form of a verb can change, for example, depending on which person is used for the subject: we say *I am* for the verb *to be* in the first person singular but *he is* for the third person singular. Whether the subject is singular or plural (grammatical number) can also affect the verb: we say *The rabbit eats* in the singular, but *The rabbits eat* in the plural. When it comes to pronouns and possessive adjectives, gender can affect which word is used: in the singular, we say *he*, *him* or *his* for the masculine, *she*, *her* or *hers* for the feminine and *it* and *its* for the neuter.

While most children use simple grammatical agreement quite naturally in their spoken and written language, it is important that they understand the principles; this will help them as they start to produce longer, more complicated writing. The idea is introduced gradually. First, the children look at what happens when certain words in a sentence are changed, starting first with object nouns and the words that describe them and then with subjects and their verbs. Then, when the children have learnt about grammatical person, they look at how changing this can affect the verb and the rest of the sentence. Encourage the children to proofread their work and to make sure that all the relevant words in the sentence agree.

Alphabetical Order, Dictionary and Thesaurus Work

Many reference materials, including dictionaries, thesauruses and encyclopedias, organise their material alphabetically. The more familiar the children are with the order of the alphabet, the better they will be at using these resources independently. In the *Grammar 1 Pupil Book*, the children were introduced to alphabetical order and to using a dictionary. To help them find words, the children were encouraged to think of the dictionary as being divided into the following four approximately equal parts:

1. **A a B b C c D d E e**
2. **F f G g H h I i J j K k L l M m**
3. **N n O o P p Q q R r S s**
4. **T t U u V v W w X x Y y Z z**

Knowing these letter groups saves the children time when using the dictionary. Before looking up a word, they decide which group its initial letter falls into, and then narrow their search to that section of the dictionary. For easy reference there is a copy of the alphabet, divided up into the four colour-coded groups, on the first page of the *Grammar 4 Pupil Book*.

The *Grammar 2 Pupil Book* improved the children's dictionary skills by teaching them to look beyond the initial letter of each word. The children practised putting into alphabetical order words that share the first two letters: for example, *sheep, shoe, ship,* and then words that share the first three letters: for example, *penny, pencil, penguin*. This skill is reinforced in the *Grammar 3* and *4 Pupil Books*, where a common activity in the spelling lessons involves putting the words from the spelling list into alphabetical order.

Most children can become quite proficient at using a dictionary designed for schools. When they finish a piece of writing, the children should proofread their work, identify any words that look incorrectly spelt and look them up in the dictionary. The children should also be encouraged to use the dictionary to look up meanings. This helps the children understand how useful dictionaries can be and aims to develop the skills they need to become regular and proficient dictionary users. In the *Grammar 2 Pupil Book*, the children practised using a dictionary to help them distinguish between homophones (such as *hear* and *here*). There is a strong focus on homophones in the *Grammar 4 Pupil Book*.

The children were also introduced to thesauruses in the *Grammar 2 Pupil Book*. (These books list words by meaning, collating words with similar meanings to one another.) The children should be encouraged to make their work more interesting by finding alternatives to words that are commonly overused, such as *nice*. In the *Grammar 4 Pupil Book*, the children learn that words with a similar meaning, which are listed in a thesaurus, are called synonyms. They also develop their knowledge of antonyms, learning that many prefixes and some suffixes can be used to create them: ‹un-›, ‹im-› and ‹non-› mean *not*; ‹de-› and ‹dis-› mean *undo* or *remove*; ‹mis-› means *wrongly* or *not*; ‹ex-› means *out* or *away from*; and ‹-less› and ‹-ful› make adjectives with the opposite meaning, indicating that the word it is describing is either *without* something or *full* of it.

It can be helpful to give each child a 'Spelling Word Book' for listing words with a particular spelling pattern and keeping a note of any homophones or unusual words they come across. These books can then be used to help the children in their independent writing. The following extension ideas are also useful for improving alphabet and dictionary skills, or for those children who finish their work ahead of time.

- The children take the words from a page of their Spelling Word Book and rewrite them in alphabetical order.
- The children use the dictionary to choose the correct spelling of a word. For this activity, write out a word three or four times on the board. Spell it slightly differently each time, but ensure that one of the spellings is correct. It is a good idea to choose a word that contains a sound with alternative spellings: for example, *disturb*, which contains the /er/ sound. This word could be spelt *disterb, distirb* or *disturb*. The children write the correct spelling in their Spelling Word Book.
- In pairs, the children race one another to find a given word in the dictionary.

Teaching Ideas for Spelling

Most children need to be taught to spell correctly. In the *Grammar Pupil Books*, spelling is the main focus for one lesson each week. The spelling activities in the *Grammar 4 Pupil Book* are designed to consolidate the children's existing knowledge, introduce new spelling patterns, and revise alternative spellings of the vowel sounds. The main focus is on words with schwas, particularly when they are in the last syllable, and on words with prefixes and suffixes.

The children first learnt to spell by listening for the sounds in a word and writing the letters that represent those sounds, and by systematically learning the spellings of key irregular, or 'tricky', words. After completing the *Phonics* and *Grammar 1 Pupil Books*, most children have a reading age of at least seven years and are starting to spell with far greater accuracy. As research has shown, children with a reading age of seven years or more are able to use analogy in their reasoning. This is a useful strategy for spelling. Children who want to write *should*, for example, might notice that the end of this word sounds like that of a word they already know, such as *would*. They could then use the spelling of *would* to write *should*, replacing the ‹w› with ‹sh›. If the children are unsure of a spelling, they may be able to find it by writing the word in several ways (e.g. *should* and 'shood'), and choosing the version that looks correct. If they have already encountered the word several times in their reading, they will probably be able to choose the right spelling. By introducing groups of spelling words that each feature a particular spelling pattern, the *Grammar Pupil Books* encourage the children to think analogically.

A focus on revising alternative spellings of vowel sounds and learning new ones helps the children consolidate and extend their learning. The alternative vowel spellings are what makes English spelling difficult and, by this stage, the children need not only to be revising the main ways of spelling the vowel sounds, but also improving their ability to remember which words take which spelling.

The *Grammar 4 Pupil Book* revises previously taught alternative spellings for the vowel sounds alongside introducing new alternative spelling patterns. This helps the children to consolidate and extend their learning. By this stage, the children need to learn the main ways of spelling each of the vowel sounds and which words take which spelling. The *Grammar 4 Pupil Book* covers the following spelling features, which are outlined in greater detail below:

1. Vowel Digraphs
2. Alternative Spellings of the Vowel Sounds
3. New Spelling Patterns
4. The Schwa
5. Syllables
6. Silent Letters
7. Identifying the Short Vowels
8. Spelling Rules

1. Vowel Digraphs

The vowel digraphs were introduced in *Phonics* and the *Grammar 1 Pupil Book*. The focus in the *Grammar 2* and *Grammar 3 Pupil Books* is on consolidating this learning. *Vowel digraph* is the term for two letters that make a single vowel sound. At least one of these letters is always a vowel. Often, the two letters are placed next to each other in a word: for example, the ‹ay› in *hay* and the ‹ew› in *few*. Two vowel letters are usually needed to make a long vowel sound. The long vowel sounds are the same as the names of the vowel letters: /ai/, /ee/, /ie/, /oa/, /ue/. Generally, the sound made by the digraph is that of the first vowel's name. Hence the well-known rule of thumb: 'When two vowels go walking, the first does the talking'.

Sometimes, the long vowel sound is made by two vowels separated by one or more consonants. In monosyllabic words, the second vowel is usually an ‹e›, known as a 'magic ‹e›' because it modifies the sound of the first vowel letter. Digraphs with a magic ‹e› can be thought of as 'hop-over ‹e›' digraphs: ‹a_e›, ‹e_e›, ‹i_e›, ‹o_e› and ‹u_e›. Once again, the sound they make is that of the first vowel's name; the 'magic ‹e›' is silent. Children like to show with their hands how the 'magic' from the ‹e› hops over the preceding consonant and changes the short vowel sound to a long one.

The hop-over ‹e› digraphs are an alternative way of making the long vowel sounds, and are found in such words as *bake, these, fine, hope* and *cube*. The children need to be shown many examples of hop-over ‹e› digraphs, which are available in the *Jolly Phonics Word Book*. It is possible to illustrate the function of the magic ‹e› in such words by using a piece of paper to cover the ‹e›, and reading the word first with the magic ‹e›, and then without it. For example, *pipe* becomes *pip* without the magic ‹e›; *hate* becomes *hat*; *hope* becomes *hop*; and *late* becomes *lat*. The children may like to do this themselves. It does not matter if, as in the *late/lat* example, they find themselves producing nonsense words; the exercise will still help them to understand the spelling rule. When looking at text on the board or in other texts, the children can be encouraged to look for and identify words with a magic ‹e›.

Although hop-over ‹e› words are generally quite common, there are only a few words with the ‹e_e› spelling pattern. Examples include: *these, scheme* and *complete*. Words with an ‹e_e› spelling are not only rather rare, but often quite advanced. For this reason, the ‹e_e› spelling is not given quite as much emphasis as the other long vowel spellings, and is not made the focus of a whole lesson until the *Grammar 3 Pupil Book*.

2. Alternative Spellings of the Vowel Sounds

Children who have learnt to read with *Jolly Phonics* are used to spelling new words by listening for the sounds and writing the letters that represent those sounds. This skill enables the children to spell accurately the many regular words that do not contain sounds with more than one spelling, words like *hot, plan, brush, drench* and *sting*.

However, words like *train, play* and *make* present a problem for spelling. All three words feature the same vowel sound: /ai/, but in each case it is spelt differently. The table opposite shows the first spelling taught for each sound and the main alternatives introduced.

First spelling taught	Alternative spellings for sound	Examples of all spellings in words
‹ai›	‹ay›, ‹a_e›	*rain, day, came*
‹ee›	‹ea›, ‹e_e›	*street, dream, these*
‹ie›	‹y›, ‹i_e›, ‹igh›	*pie, by, time, light*
‹oa›	‹ow›, ‹o_e›	*boat, snow, home*
‹ue›	‹ew›, ‹u_e›	*due, few, cube*
‹er›	‹ir›, ‹ur›	*her, first, turn*
‹oi›	‹oy›	*boil, toy*
‹ou›	‹ow›	*out, cow*
‹or›	‹al›, ‹au›, ‹aw›	*for, sauce, talk, saw*

The alternative spellings of vowel sounds were introduced in the *Grammar 1 Pupil Book* and then revised in the *Grammar 2* and *3 Pupil Books*, and should be familiar to the children. The alternative vowel spellings are what make English spelling difficult and it is very important to further consolidate this teaching. This can be achieved by revising the spelling patterns regularly with flash cards, and by asking the children to list the alternative spellings for a particular sound. The children should be able to do this automatically and apply their knowledge when writing unfamiliar words. For example, with a word like *frame*, they should be able to write 'fraim, fraym, frame' on a scrap of paper, before deciding which version looks correct.

3. New Spelling Patterns

Many of the less common spellings of familiar sounds are introduced in the *Grammar 2, 3* and *4 Pupil Books*. The tables opposite show the spellings first taught, and the new spelling patterns introduced.

The children need to memorise which words use each of these new spelling patterns. It is helpful to make up silly sentences for each spelling, using as many of the words as possible. For example, for the ‹ie› spelling of the /ee/ sound, the children could chant the following: *I believe my niece was the chief thief who came to grief over the piece of shield she hid in the field.*

In the *Grammar 2* and *Grammar 3 Pupil Books*, the children learnt some new sounds that were not included in the *Phonics* and *Grammar 1 Pupil Books*. For example, in the *Grammar 2 Pupil Book*, the /ear/ sound was introduced initially as ‹ear›, as in *hear* and *earrings*. In the *Grammar 3 Pupil Book*, the children learnt the alternative spellings, ‹eer› and ‹ere›, as in *deer* and *cheer*, and *here* and *mere*. Similarly, the /air/ sound was introduced initially as ‹air›, ‹are› and ‹ear›, as in *hair*, *care* and *bear*. The *Grammar 3 Pupil Book* taught the ‹ere› spelling, as in *there*, *ere* and *where*. The children's knowledge of ‹ure› was also revised and extended in the *Grammar 3 Pupil Book*. The children revise the /cher/ sound made by ‹ture› in a word like *picture*, and learn that ‹ure› often follows ‹s› to make words like *pleasure* and *treasure*, where the ‹s› makes a /zh/ sound. The ‹ure› spelling pattern can also follow other letters to make words like *figure*, *failure* and *conjure*.

4. The Schwa

In the *Grammar 4 Pupil Book*, the children are introduced to the schwa, which is the most common vowel sound in English. It is used when the vowel in an unstressed syllable is swallowed and loses its purity, becoming more like an /uh/ sound.

Although it is the most common vowel sound, the schwa is not taught earlier because it can be made by any unstressed vowel. This means that there is no helpful spelling rule for the children to use and so the spellings have to be learnt. Instead, encourage the children to 'say it as it sounds', stressing the pure form of the schwa and saying, for example, 'doct-or' rather than 'doct-uh'. This is a useful strategy for any word that is difficult to spell.

5. Syllables

An understanding of syllables will help to improve the children's spelling. A number of spelling rules depend on the children's ability to identify the number of syllables in a given word. Knowing about syllables will also help the children later on when they begin to learn about where the stress

First spelling taught for sound(s)	New spelling(s) for sound(s)	Examples of new spellings in words
Spellings taught in the *Grammar 2 Pupil Book*		
‹ai›	‹ei›, ‹eigh›	*veil, eighteen*
cher*	‹ture›	*capture, nature*
‹e›	‹ea›	*breakfast, ready*
‹ee›	‹ey›, ‹ie›, ‹y›	*key, field, fairy*
‹f›	‹ph›	*graph, photo*
‹j›	'soft' ‹g›	*gem, giant*
‹k›	‹ch›, ‹ck›	*chord, cricket*
ool*	‹-le›	*handle, little*
‹or›	‹ore›	*more, snore, wore*
‹s›	'soft' ‹c›	*cell, city, cycle*
‹shun›*	‹sion›, ‹tion›	*tension, station*
‹u›	‹o›, ‹ou›	*month, touch*
‹w›	‹wh›	*whale, whistle*
‹(w)o›	‹(w)a›	*swan, watch, was*
‹zhun›*	‹sion›	*division, occasion*
Spellings taught in the *Grammar 3 Pupil Book*		
‹ai›	‹a›	*able, taste, haste*
‹air›, ‹are›, ‹ear›	‹ere›	*where, there*
‹ar›	‹a›	*koala, vase, lava*
‹ch›	‹tch›	*match, itch, fetch*
‹ear›*	‹eer›, ‹ere›	*cheer, deer, here*
‹ee›	‹e›, ‹e_e›	*athlete, secret*
‹f›	‹gh›	*enough, cough*
‹i›	‹y›	*myth, pyramid*
‹ie›	‹i›	*child, wild*
‹j›	‹dge›	*edge, bridge, judge*
‹n›	‹gn›	*gnome, resign*
‹ng›	‹n›	*trunk, finger*
‹oa›	‹o›	*only, ogre, ago*
‹o› (after ‹qu›)	‹a› (after ‹qu›)	*squad, quantity*
‹ue›	‹u›	*menu, emu*
‹z›	‹s›, ‹se›, ‹ze›	*easy, pause, bronze*
Spellings taught in the *Grammar 4 Pupil Book*		
‹er›	‹ear›	*earth, pearl*
‹g›	‹gh›	*ghost, aghast*
‹oo›	‹u›	*truth, flu*
‹or›	‹ough›, ‹augh›	*ought, caught*
‹s›	‹se›, ‹st›	*goose, listen*
‹v›	‹ve›	*solve, curve*
‹(w)er›	‹(w)or›	*worm, worker*

* As the relevant lesson plans explain, this is only an approximation of the sound made by the new spelling.

is placed in words. Although the rules of English sometimes let us down, they are worth acquiring. The more the children know, the more skilful they become, and the better equipped they are to deal with any irregularities.

In the *Grammar 2 Pupil Book* the children were encouraged to count the syllables in words using 'chin bumps'. Chin bumps are a fun, multisensory way of teaching syllables. The children place one hand under their chin (with the hand flattened as though they are about to pat something). Then they slowly say a word, and count the number of times they feel their chin go down and bump on their hand. For *cat*, for example, they will feel one bump, which means it has one syllable. *Table* has two bumps, so two syllables; *any* has two bumps and two syllables; *screeched* has one bump and one syllable; and *idea* has three bumps and three syllables.

In the *Grammar 3* and *4 Pupil Books*, the teaching of syllables is extended and refined. In the *Grammar 3 Pupil Book*, the children learn that syllables are units of sound organised around the vowel sounds. If a word has three vowel sounds, for example, it will have three syllables. (Words with three or more syllables are referred to as multisyllabic, or polysyllabic.) If a word only has one vowel sound, and therefore one syllable, it is called a monosyllabic word. The *Grammar 4 Pupil Book* introduces the idea that, in English, stress is placed on at least one of the syllables in a multisyllabic word. The children also learn that a vowel in an unstressed syllable can lose its pure sound and become a schwa.

The children are given regular practice identifying the syllables in words. They will find doing this aurally (using chin bumps or by clapping the syllables) quite easy with practice. The children are also encouraged to identify syllables on paper, by underlining the letters making the vowel sounds and then drawing a vertical line between the syllables. There are some simple rules the children can learn to help them split words with double consonants, or with ‹ck› and ‹le› spellings:

- **Double consonants**: when a consonant is doubled, the line goes between them, as in *kit/ten*. However, the children should take care with words like *hopped*, *stopped* and *nipped*, where the ‹e› in ‹-ed› is silent. These may look like two-syllable words but they are, in fact, monosyllabic.
- **‹ck› words**: although ‹c› and ‹k› make the same sound and so act like double consonants, the line goes after the ‹k›, as in *pock/et*.
- **‹le› words**: the sounds represented by the ‹le› spelling are the same as those for ‹el› and ‹il› and consist of a small schwa before the /l/. This swallowed vowel sound can clearly be seen in *label* and *pencil* but not in *candle*: in ‹le› words there is no written vowel to underline in the last syllable. Instead, when the children see a word like this, they must listen for the schwa and draw a line before the consonant preceding it, as in *can/dle* and *sad/dle*. Again, ‹ck› words are an exception; the line goes after the ‹k›, as in *pick/le*, *cack/le* and *buck/le*.

Exactly how a word is split into syllables often depends on whether the syllable is 'open' or 'closed'. Open syllables are syllables ending in a long vowel sound, and closed syllables are syllables with a short vowel that end in a consonant. The type of syllable is not always easy to determine, as many long vowels become swallowed and are pronounced as schwas in English. The guidance given in the lesson plans aims to follow these rules, but in practice there is no definitive way to split the syllables and different dictionaries will often do it in different ways. For now, the focus should be on improving the children's ability to identify the vowel sounds in a word and hear how many syllables there are.

6. Silent Letters

A number of English words contain letters that are not pronounced at all. These are known as silent letters. Some silent letters, such as the ‹k› in *knee*, show us how the word was pronounced in the past. Other silent letters, like the ‹h› in *rhyme*, indicate the word's foreign origins. The *Grammar Pupil Books* introduce the following silent letters:

- silent ‹b›, as in *lamb*
- silent ‹c›, as in *scissors*
- silent ‹h›, as in *rhubarb*

- silent ‹k›, as in *knife*
- silent ‹w›, as in *wrong*
- silent ‹g›, as in *gnome*
- silent ‹t›, as in *castle*.

The *Grammar 2 Pupil Book* introduced the first five silent letters. The *Grammar 3 Pupil Book* introduced silent ‹g› as part of the spelling pattern ‹gn›, which says the /n/ sound. The *Grammar 4 Pupil Book* introduces silent ‹t› as part of the spelling pattern ‹st›. Practising with the 'say it as it sounds' technique helps children remember these spellings. For the word *lamb*, for example, say the word to the class, pronouncing it correctly as /lam/. The children respond by saying /lamb/, emphasising the /b/. The *Grammar 4 Pupil Book* teaches the children that some silent letters often go with a particular letter, as in ‹mb›, ‹wr›, ‹kn›, ‹wh›, ‹rh›, ‹wh›, ‹sc›, ‹gh›, ‹st› and ‹gn›. They are encouraged to think of these as silent letter digraphs.

7. Identifying the Short Vowels

One of the most reliable spelling rules in English is the consonant doubling rule. Consonant doubling is governed by the short vowels, so the children need to be able to identify short vowel sounds confidently. In the *Grammar 1* and *Grammar 2 Pupil Books*, a puppet was used to encourage the children to listen for the short vowels.

- For /a/, put the puppet at the side of the box.
- For /e/, make the puppet wobble on the edge of the box.
- For /i/, put the puppet in the box.
- For /o/, put the puppet on the box.
- For /u/, put the puppet under the box.

The children pretended that their fist was the box and their hand was the puppet. Initially, the children were encouraged to do the appropriate action when the short vowel sounds were called out. Then, they learnt to do the actions when they heard short words with a short vowel sound (e.g. *pot, hat, bun, dig, red*). Once the children had learnt to distinguish between short vowels and long vowels (and the other vowel sounds) they were able to do the appropriate short vowel action when short words with a variety of vowel sounds were called out. For those that did not have a short vowel sound, the children kept their hands still.

The children are encouraged to revise the short vowel sounds regularly using the vowel hand. They hold up one hand so their palm is facing them; then, using the index finger of the other hand, they point to the tip of each finger, saying the vowel sounds in turn. First they point to the tip of the thumb for /a/, then to the first finger for /e/, and so on. Then, as they revise the long vowel sounds, they can point to the base of each finger as they say /ai/, /ee/, /ie/, /oa/ and /ue/.

Activities like these help to keep the children tuned in to identifying the sounds in words and, in turn, help to prepare them for the consonant doubling rules.

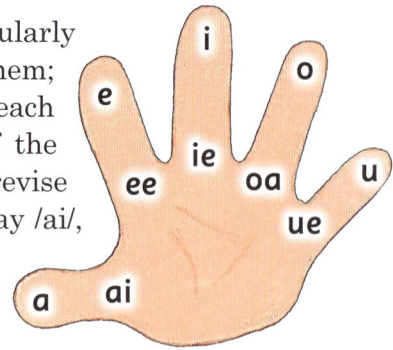

8. Spelling Rules

An ability to identify syllables and short vowels will help the children apply the following rules for consonant doubling and adding suffixes.

Spelling Rules for Consonant Doubling

a. In a monosyllabic word with a short vowel sound, ending in ‹f›, ‹l›, ‹s› or ‹z›, the final consonant letter is doubled, as in the words *cliff, bell, miss* and *buzz*. (The only exceptions to this rule include the tricky two-letter words: *as, if, is, of* and *us*.)

b. In a monosyllabic word with a short vowel sound, if the last consonant sound is /k/, this is spelt ‹ck›, as in the words: *back, neck, lick, clock* and *duck*.

c. If there is only one consonant after a short, stressed vowel sound, this consonant is doubled before any suffix starting with a vowel is added. For example, when the suffixes ‹-ed›, ‹-er›, ‹-est›, ‹-ing›, ‹-y› and ‹-able› are added to the words *hop, wet, big, clap, fun* and *hug*, the final consonants are doubled so that we get *hopped, wetter, biggest, clapping, funny* and *huggable*. Note that when ‹y› is a suffix, it counts as a vowel because it has a vowel sound. (This rule does not apply to those words where the final consonant is ‹x›, because ‹x› is really the two consonant sounds /k/ and /s/. This means that ‹x› is never doubled, even in words like *faxed, boxing* and *mixer*.) It can help if the children think of the two consonants as forming a 'wall'. If there were only one consonant, the wall would not be thick enough to prevent 'magic' hopping over from the vowel in the suffix and changing the short vowel sound to a long one. With two consonants, the wall becomes so thick that the 'magic' cannot get over (see Spelling Rules for Adding Suffixes, rule e).

d. When a word ends with the letters ‹le› and the preceding syllable contains a short, stressed vowel sound, there must be two consonants between the short vowel and the ‹-le›. This means that the consonant before the ‹-le› is doubled in words like *paddle, kettle, nibble, topple* and *snuggle*. No doubling is necessary in words like *handle, twinkle* and *jungle* because they already have two consonants between the short vowel and the ‹le›.

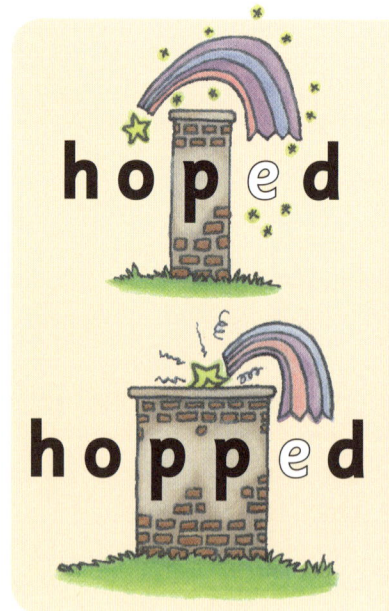

Spelling Rules for Adding Suffixes

a. If the root word ends with a consonant that is not immediately preceded by a short vowel sound, simply add the suffix. So, *walk* + ‹-ed› = *walked, quick* + ‹-est› = *quickest, look* + ‹-ing› = *looking* and *avoid* + ‹-able› = *avoidable*.

b. If the root word ends with the letter ‹e› and the suffix starts with a vowel, remove the ‹e› before adding the suffix. So, *love* + ‹-ed› = *loved, brave* + ‹-er› = *braver, like* + ‹-ing› = *liking* and *value* + ‹-able› = *valuable,* but *care* + ‹-less› = *careless.*

The main exception to this rule is when the suffix ‹-ing› is added to a root word that has an ‹i› before the ‹e›, as in *tie.* To avoid having two ‹i›s next to each other (e.g. 'tiing'), both the ‹i› and the ‹e› are replaced with a ‹y›. So *tie* + ‹-ing› = *tying* and *lie* + ‹-ing› = *lying,* even though these same words become *tied* and *lied* when adding ‹-ed›. Another exception is when the ‹e› is part of the soft ‹c› or soft ‹g› spelling and the suffix ‹-able› is added. In this instance, the ‹e› is kept so that ‹c› is pronounced /s/ and ‹g› is pronounced /j/, as in *noticeable* and *changeable.* (Some words can be spelt either with or without the ‹e›, so both *lovable* and *loveable* are correct; however, in these cases it is better for the children to be consistent and drop the ‹e› in their writing.)

c. If the root word ends in ‹ce› or ‹ge› and the suffix is ‹-able›, do not remove the ‹e›. This is because the ‹e› is part of the soft ‹c› and ‹g› spellings, making the ‹c› say /s/ and the ‹g› say /j/, as in *noticeable* and *changeable.*

d. If the root word ends in ‹ce› and the suffix is ‹-al›, replace ‹e› with ‹i› before adding the suffix. So *commerce* + ‹-al› = *commercial.*

e. If the root word ends with a consonant that is immediately preceded by a short, stressed vowel sound and the suffix begins with a vowel, double the final consonant before adding the suffix. So, *stop* + ‹-ed› = *stopped, sad* + ‹-er› = *sadder, run* + ‹-ing› = *running* and *control* + ‹-able› = *controllable,* but *sad* + ‹-ness› = *sadness,*

Remind the children that two consonants are needed to make a 'wall', to prevent 'magic' from the vowel in the suffix from jumping over to change the short vowel sound. (See: Spelling Rules for Consonant Doubling, rule c.)

f. If the root word ends with the letter ‹y›, which is immediately preceded by a consonant, replace the ‹y› with an ‹i› before adding the suffix. So, *hurry* + ‹-ed› = *hurried, dirty* + ‹-est› = *dirtiest, beauty* + ‹-ful› = *beautiful, vary* + ‹-able› = *variable* and *pity* + ‹-ful› = *pitiful.* However, if the suffix starts with the letter ‹i›, the rule does not apply, so *worry* + ‹-ing› = *worrying.*

The letter ‹y› is unique in being able to function as either a vowel or a consonant. As a vowel, ‹y› replaces ‹i›. In the *Phonics Pupil Books,* the children learnt that 'shy ‹i›' does not like to go at the end of a word, so 'toughy ‹y›' takes its place. As the last syllable of a multisyllabic word, the sound ‹y› makes is somewhere between the short /i/ in *tin* and the long /ee/ in *bee.* (This is also true of the rare instances when the letter ‹i› is the final syllable of a polysyllabic word, as in *taxi.*) Despite this confusing pronunciation, it is important for the children to think of ‹y› as replacing 'shy ‹i›'. This will help them remember that the ‹i› returns when such words are extended (except in words like *worrying,* where it would look odd to have two ‹i›s next to each other).

In the *Grammar Pupil Books,* suffixes and prefixes are taught with prefix and suffix fish. Prefixes are shown on the fish's head; the root (or *base*) word is shown on the fish's body and suffixes are shown on fish tails (see illustration opposite).

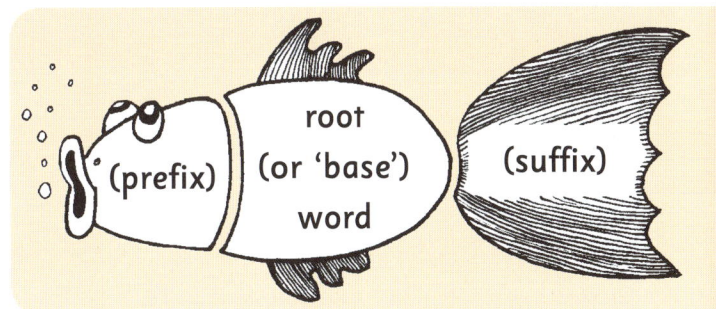

Spelling and Grammar Lessons

For each lesson, there is an activity page in the *Pupil Book* for the children to complete and an accompanying lesson plan in the *Teacher's Book*. The recommendations in the teacher's lesson plans are intended to be followed systematically. However, if a suggestion seems inappropriate for a particular class situation, it can of course be adapted to suit.

Each lesson plan also features a reduced copy of the relevant activity page in the *Pupil Book*. It can be helpful to refer to this prior to, or during, the lesson.

Grammar Lessons

Each grammar lesson has its own particular focus and the lesson plans vary accordingly. Despite this, the grammar lessons all follow the same standard format, which helps to give them a recognisable shape. The format of the grammar lessons is as follows.

a. Aim
b. Introduction
c. Main Point
d. Activity Page
e. Extension Activity
f. Rounding Off

Spelling Lessons

The spelling lessons all follow the same basic format.

a. Spelling Test
b. Revision
c. Spelling Point
d. Spelling List
e. Activity Page
f. Dictation
g. Extension Activity

Many teaching points are common to all of the spelling lessons, so these are explained in further detail on the following pages.

a. Spelling Test

Six pages have been provided at the back of the *Grammar 4 Pupil Book* for the children's spelling tests (pages 74 to 79).

Start by telling the children to turn to the back of their books and find the space for that particular week's spelling test. Call out the words one at a time for the children to write on the lines. Repeat each word twice, giving the children just enough time to write each word before moving on to the next one. The words can be called out in the same order as they appear in the list, but it is best if they are called out in a random order. Those children who are finding it difficult can be given fewer words to learn.

b. Revision

Each lesson should start with a short burst of revision. To begin with, the revision sessions concentrate on the consonant digraphs and the five vowel letters, specifically their short and long sounds and their main alternative spellings. This revision can be carried out using vowel hands (see page 24, Identifying the Short Vowels) and either flash cards or the *Jolly Phonics Alternative Spelling Poster*. The children also practise identifying syllables in words, either by clapping or doing chin bumps (see page 22). Over the course of the year, teachers can add other areas to this revision, including the spelling patterns introduced or revised in recent lessons. Particular attention should be given to schwas, prefixes and suffixes. A list of suitable words is suggested, which can be written on the board and discussed with the class.

c. Spelling Point

A number of the spelling lessons in the *Grammar 4 Pupil Book* introduce a completely new spelling pattern, but mainly they are concerned with refining the children's spelling ability. The main focus is on words with schwas, particularly when they are in the last syllable, and on words with prefixes and suffixes.

Pupil Book page	Word bank
2. ‹ch›, ‹sh›, ‹th›	*cheese, branch, lunchbox, shoes, fresh, accomplish, thirteen, teeth, beneath*
4. Homophones	*eye, I, know, no, deer, dear, it's, its, ewe, you, son, sun, one, won, tail, tale, see, sea*
6. ‹nch›	*bench, munch, bunch, finch, trench, brunch, punch, French, inch, stench*
8. ‹se› saying /s/	*false, mouse, course, expense, intense, briefcase, greenhouse, bookcase, decrease*
10. ‹ve› saying /v/	*give, halve, delve, active, festive, adjective, detective, illusive, competitive*
12. Plurals: ‹ves›	*caves, chives, gloves, groves, nerves, slaves, sleeves, olives, airwaves, beehives,*
14. Schwa ‹a›	*about, alone, again, arrive, sofa, koala, pentagon, attention, pleasant, paragraph*
16. Schwa ‹o›	*occur, offend, seldom, London, confront, condition, melody, biology, professional*
18. Schwa ‹u›	*awful, cheerful, circus, locust, supply, succumb, support, calcium, education*
20. Schwa ‹ar›	*altar, collar, awkward, backward, lizard, coward, polar, cellar, blizzard*
22. Schwa ‹or›	*anchor, censor, factor, monitor, creator, alligator, temporary, collaborate*
24. Schwa ‹er›	*lantern, energy, allergy, better, after, power, matter, together, partnership*

Pupil Book page	Word bank
26. ‹or› saying /er/	*work, worth, network, password, artwork, framework, wordplay, trustworthy*
28. ‹ear› saying /er/	*earlier, learning, earned, research, unearthed, searched, yearning*
30. ‹u› saying long /oo/	*gruel, druid, ruined, supreme, truthful, affluent, superlative*
32. ‹ough›, ‹gh›, ‹augh›	*sought, overwrought; ghostwriter, ghoulish; haughty, taught*
34. ‹ive› saying /iv/	*give, native, captive, creative, deceptive, offensive, impulsive, talkative, sensitive*
36. ‹-ic›	*basic, music, cosmic, cryptic, fabric, electric, acidic, allergic, diabetic, electronic*
38. ‹st› saying /s/	*hustle, rustle, trestle, christen, listened, fastened, wrestled, apostle, epistle*
40. Silent Letters	*w**h**istle, **w**hip; **w**rench, **w**riting; **k**nife, **k**neecap; lam**b**, thum**b**; **sc**ene, **sc**ience*
42. ‹-ically›	*practically, musically, tragically, whimsically, magically, publically, physically*
44. Schwa ‹al›	*fin**al**, soci**al**, norm**al**, arriv**al**, factu**al**, coloss**al**, diagon**al**, origin**al**, addition**al***
46. Schwa ‹el›	*ang**el**, bag**el**, jew**el**, pan**el**, satch**el**, quarr**el**, flann**el**, parc**el**, squirr**el**, swiv**el***
48. Schwa ‹il›	*dev**il**, dev**il**ish, nostr**il**s, penc**il**s, lent**il**s, tendr**il**s, unciv**il**, per**il**ous, tranqu**il**ity*
50. ‹-ery›	*every, battery, celery, robbery, cookery, misery, feathery, recovery, embroidery*
52. ‹-ary›	*burglary, dietary, legendary, military, rosemary, secondary, stationary, sugary*
54. ‹-ory›	*glory, memory, ivory, accessory, auditory, directory, predatory, multisensory*
56. ‹-ant›	*assistant, confidant, constant, defiant, elegant, flippant, important, tolerant*
58. ‹-ent›	*dent, lent, rent, scent, urgent, comment, consent, accident, different, document*
60. ‹-ist›	*fist, list, mist, wrist, dentist, florist, persist, resist, activist, motorist, pianist*
62. ‹pre-›	*prefer, precaution, preclude, predate, preempt, preheat, prelude, prepaid, preference*
64. ‹sub-›	*subject, subset, subsist, subtext, subtotal, subsidy, subcategory, subculture*
66. ‹anti-›	*anticipate, antipathy, antique, antiquity, antiquated, antiviral, antiviolence*
68. ‹trans-›	*transcribe, transcript, transfix, transform, translator, transmission*
70. ‹inter-›	*intern, internal, interaction, intercom, interest, interfere, interior, interlink*
72. ‹tele-›	*telecommunications, telemarketer, teleology, teleportation, telescopic*

These words could be used as the starting point for the children's word lists in their Spelling Word Books (see g. Extension Activity, page 30).

d. Spelling List

Each week, the children are given eighteen words with a particular spelling pattern to learn for a test. It is a good idea to give the spelling homework at the beginning of the week and to test at the end of the week, or on the following Monday.

     The spelling words have been carefully selected to enable every child to have some success. The eighteen words are arranged on the *Pupil Book* pages in three groups of six. The words in the first group are usually short, regular and fairly common; those in the second group are a bit longer and may have more alternative spellings in them; and the third group has longer, often less common words, with more varied spellings.

For those children who find spelling difficult, it may be appropriate to give them only the first six spelling words; the number can be increased when the children are ready. The number of spelling words given to the children is at the teacher's discretion, based on his or her knowledge of the children in the class.

It is important to go over the words during the spelling lesson. Look carefully at each spelling list with the class; discuss the meanings of any unfamiliar words; and look to see which parts of a word are regular and identify those parts that are not. The lesson plans in the *Teacher's Book* point out the words that need particular attention and suggest suitable learning strategies. The spelling activity pages will also help the children become more familiar with the words and their spellings. Go over the spelling words as often as possible during the week, ideally, blending and sounding out the words with the children every day.

Each child takes the list of spellings home to learn. If the children usually leave their *Pupil Books* at school, the words can be copied out into a small homework book for the children to take home. If the children do the writing, check that they have copied the words clearly and accurately before the books go home.

Test and mark the spellings each week. The results should be written in the children's *Pupil Books* for the parents to see. The marks can be shown either as a mark out of eighteen, or with a coded system if preferred. For example, a coloured star system might be used, with a gold star for 18/18, a silver star for 17/18 and a coloured star for 16/18. Most parents like to be involved in their children's homework, and are interested to see how many words their child spelt correctly and which words were misspelt.

Children need to be aware that accurate spelling is important for their future. Unfortunately, there is no magic wand that can be waved to make them good at spelling. In addition to knowing the letter sounds and alternative spellings thoroughly, a certain amount of dedication and practice is needed.

e. Activity Page

The focus of each spelling page reflects the main teaching point. Every week, the first of the activities requires the children to use the words from the spelling list. The children could, for example, be asked to fill in missing letters, solve anagrams, complete a word search, match the spelling words to their descriptions, use the words to complete sentences, put words into alphabetical order, correct misspellings, write the meanings of the spelling words or use them in a sentence. These activities allow the children to engage actively with the spelling words, which makes learning the words more meaningful.

The second activity often gives the children the opportunity to work with some of the spelling words in a grammar context: for example, they might be asked to practise syllables, plurals and punctuation, or extend their word knowledge with homophones, antonyms, synonyms, comparatives and superlatives.

Lastly, the children are asked to identify the subject of a simple sentence, which they then parse (underlining the parts of speech in the appropriate colour). It is best if children start with the nouns and verbs, as most other parts of speech relate to these in one way or another. For some children, simply finding the nouns and verbs may be sufficient. From early on, the children are asked to identify the verb's tense, and later they must also choose the correct grammatical person (deciding whether the sentence is written in the first, second or third person and whether the person is singular or plural).

f. Dictation

As a weekly exercise, dictation is useful in a number of ways. It gives the children regular practice listening for the sounds in the words they write, and is a good way of monitoring their progress. Dictation helps the children to develop their independent writing and encourages the slower writers to increase their speed. It also provides a good opportunity for the children to practise their punctuation, such as commas, speech marks and question and exclamation marks. The dictation sections in each lesson plan suggest the important things to point out to the children.

There are three sentences each week for dictation. All of the sentences revise the spelling focus for that week, and may also feature spelling patterns and grammar points from previous lessons. For example, when the spelling focus is ‹gh›, ‹ough› and ‹augh›, the dictation sentences feature words like *ought* and *daughter*, but they also revise recently learnt spellings such as ‹ear› for /er/, as in *search* and *earth*, and ‹u› for long /oo/, as in *flu*.

Begin by calling out the first sentence for the children to write down. Give the children a reasonable amount of time to finish writing, but not too long, and then move on to the next sentence. The few children who have not yet finished should leave the sentence incomplete and move on. This encourages them to get up to speed. Afterwards, it is important to go over the sentences with the children and discuss the spellings, grammar and punctuation points.

g. Extension Activity

The lesson notes also outline an extension activity for most of the spelling lessons. Some of the extension activities are included on the activity book pages, but most will need to be completed on a separate sheet of paper. Some activities will require words or sentences to be written on the board as a starting point for the children. Each activity focuses on the weekly spelling pattern, provides further practice on a related grammar point or combines the two: examples include homophones, antonyms and synonyms, plurals, root words, prefixes and suffixes, comparatives and superlatives, possessive nouns and punctuation.

It is useful for the children to have their own little Spelling Word Book. Every week, the children can collect words with the week's spelling pattern, starting with the words from the spelling list and adding more as they think of them. They can then use their Spelling Word Book to look back at the spellings they have learnt or check how they should be written. As a further extension activity, they could also work in pairs and go through the books, testing each other on the spellings.

PART 2

Teaching with the Grammar 4 Pupil Book

The following pages provide detailed lesson plans and teaching guidance for use alongside the activity pages in the *Grammar 4 Pupil Book*. It is a good idea to read through the relevant teaching guidance prior to each lesson, and to prepare any additional materials that might be required.

For a typical spelling lesson, the teacher will need to prepare flash cards for the revision session, as well as coloured pens or pencils, highlighters, paper and dictionaries for the children's use. The teacher may also find it helpful to prepare a list of words featuring the spelling pattern(s) of the week prior to the lesson. (The word banks on pages 27 and 28 can be used as a starting point for this list.) The requirements for the grammar lessons are more varied. As for the spelling lessons, every grammar lesson requires the children to have access to dictionaries, thesauruses, and coloured pens or pencils. A number of the extension activities also require lined paper for extended writing and art and craft materials for creating wall displays.

Spelling: ‹ch›, ‹sh› and ‹th›

Spelling Test
- As the children have not been given any spelling words to learn yet, there is no spelling test in this lesson.

Revision
- Revise the consonant digraphs: ‹ng›, ‹ch›, ‹sh›, ‹th›, ‹qu›; the vowel digraphs: ‹or›, ‹oo›, ‹ow›, ‹oi›, ‹er›, ‹ar›; the short vowel sounds, /a/, /e/, /i/, /o/, /u/; and the various spellings of the long vowel sounds: /ai/ ‹ai›, ‹ay›, ‹a_e›; /ee/ ‹ee›, ‹ea›, ‹e_e›; /ie/ ‹ie›, ‹y›, ‹igh›, ‹i_e›; /oa/ ‹oa›, ‹ow›, ‹o_e›; /ue/ ‹ue›, ‹ew›, ‹u_e›. Flash cards can be used for reading and sound dictation for spelling.
- These are sounds and spellings that the children should know well by now, so if anyone in the class is unsure about them, time should be taken during the week to go over the digraphs.

Spelling Point
- Revise blending sounds to read words and sounding out words to spell them. Remind the children that words can be broken down into syllables, which are units of sound containing a vowel sound. Explain that doing this can help them with their spelling, particularly of longer words.
- Write a few words on the board, including some with double consonants, ‹ck› and ‹le›, and remind the children how to first identify the vowel sound(s) and then split the words into syllables with a line.

Spelling List
- Read the spelling words with the children, explain any words they may not know, and ask them to find and highlight the ‹ch›, ‹sh› and ‹th› digraphs.
- Make sure that the children understand when to use ‹ck› and ‹k›, as in *backlash* and *benchmark* (see Spelling Rules, page 24), how the 'magic' in a vowel can change the preceding short vowel sound into a long one, as in *betrothed*, and the spelling rules for adding suffixes, as in *faithful* and *loathing* (see page 25).
- Remind them that when ‹y› is on the end of words like *thorny* and *anchovy* it says /ee/, and that the /ai/ sound on the end of a word is often spelt ‹ay›, as in *archway*.
- Point out the ‹ie› spelling of /ee/ in *achieve*, the soft ‹g› in *gibberish*, the ‹y› saying /i/ in *mythical* and the ‹a› spelling of /o/ when it follows the /w/ sound in *squashed*.

smooth
famish
thorny
loathing
backlash
cheerless
benchmark
archway
bashful
faithful
outlandish
parchment
gibberish
mythical
achieve
anchovy
squashed
betrothed

Activity Page
- The children add the missing digraphs, ‹ch›, ‹sh› or ‹th›, to complete the words. Then they look at the words in the logs, underline the letters making the vowel sounds and separate the words into syllables with a line (*out/land/ish*, *cheer/less*, *gib/ber/ish*, *fam/ish*, *bash/ful*, *thorn/y*).
- Finally, the children parse the sentence, underlining each part of speech in the correct colour, and identify the subject (*I*). Point out that *fishy* is an adjective made by adding the suffix ‹-y› to the noun *fish* and that *my* is a possessive adjective describing who the pizza belongs to.

I loathe fishy anchovy on my pizza.

Dictation
- Provide a sheet of paper for each child and dictate the following sentences:

1. The chimpanzee was talking a lot of gibberish.
2. The Viking longship was vanishing into the distance.
3. Both of the girls wished for good weather.

Extension Activity
- Provide a sheet of paper for each child.
- Each child draws three columns: one for ‹ch›, one for ‹sh› and one for ‹th›. The children then write the words from the activities in the correct columns.

Grammar: Verb Tenses

Aim
· Revise the simple and continuous tenses learnt in the previous three years.

Introduction
· Write *to cook* on the board and ask what sort of word *cook* is (a verb). When a verb has *to* in front of it, it is called the infinitive. Verbs describe what is happening in the past, present or future and they can be written in the simple and continuous tenses.
· Draw a simple grid of six boxes on the board and write in the tenses as you talk about them (each box should be large enough for a simple sentence).
· Discuss how the tenses are formed (see Verbs, pages 9 to 11): sometimes adding a suffix like ‹-ed› or ‹-ing›, sometimes by using an auxiliary like *shall* or *will*, and sometimes by adding both.
· Remind the children that when ‹-ing› is added to the verb it is called the present participle and that this form of the verb, along with the auxiliary verb *to be*, is used to make the continuous tenses.
· Conjugate the irregular verb *to be* with the class in the simple present, past and future, doing the pronoun actions.

Main Point
· Say *I cook lunch* and ask which tense the sentence is in (the simple present). Write it in the correct box. Call out the same sentence in another tense for the children to identify. Continue to do this, using all six tenses. Remind the children of the spelling rules for adding ‹-ed› and ‹-ing› (see Spelling Rules, pages 24 to 25).

	Simple	Continuous
Past	I cooked lunch.	I was cooking lunch.
Present	I cook lunch.	I am cooking lunch.
Future	I shall/will cook lunch.	I shall/will be cooking lunch.

· Remind the class that the simple present describes an action that is repeated or usual: e.g. *I cook every day*; while the present continuous describes something that has started and is still happening: e.g. *I am cooking dinner*.
· The simple past describes an action that started and finished within a specific time: e.g. *I cooked a meal today*; while the continuous past describes an action that had started and was still happening in the past: *I was cooking dinner when they called*.
· Similarly, the simple future describes an action that will start and finish within a specific time: e.g. *I will cook tonight*; while the continuous future describes an action that will start and still be happening in the future: *I will be cooking dinner later*.

Activity Page
· The children write inside the outlined word *Verbs*, using a red pencil. They then read each sentence, decide which tense is being used, and match it to the correct tense in the tense tents.
· Finally, the children write the sentences in the six tenses they know: *Meg will hum a tune*; *Meg was humming a tune*; *Meg is humming a tune*; *Meg will be humming a tune*; *You juggled brilliantly*; *You will juggle brilliantly*; *You were juggling brilliantly*; *You are juggling brilliantly*; *You will be juggling brilliantly*.

Extension Activity
· Provide a sheet of paper for each child.
· The children practise writing more sentences in the six tenses they know. Give each child a simple sentence as a starting point: for example, *She sketches a portrait*; *He plays the drums*; *I follow the instructions*; *They grin at each other*; *We dance every week*; *Jack bounces the ball*. It is better to give them sentences, rather than ask them to make them up; this will avoid irregular verbs and complex sentences.

Rounding Off
· Go over the activity page with the children, checking their answers. If they have done the extension activity, ask some of the children to read out their sentences.

Spelling: Homophones

Spelling Test
- The children turn to the backs of their books and find the column labelled *Spelling Test 1*.
- In any order, call out the spelling words learnt last week. The children write the words on the lines.

Revision
- Revise the consonant digraphs: ‹ng›, ‹ch›, ‹sh›, ‹th›, ‹qu›; the vowel digraphs: ‹or›, ‹oo›, ‹ou›, ‹oi›, ‹er›, ‹ar›; the five short vowels, /a/, /e/, /i/, /o/, /u/; and the different spellings of the long vowel sounds: /ai/ ‹ai›, ‹ay›, ‹a_e›; /ee/ ‹ee›, ‹ea›, ‹e_e›; /ie/ ‹ie›, ‹y›, ‹igh›, ‹i_e›; /oa/ ‹oa›, ‹ow›, ‹o_e›; /ue/ ‹ue›, ‹ew›, ‹u_e›. Flash cards can be used for reading and sound dictation for spelling.

Spelling Point
- Remind the children that homophones are words that sound similar to one another but have different spellings and meanings. *Homophone* comes from the Greek *homo*, meaning *same*, and *phone*, meaning *sound*.
- Remind them that it is very important to use the correct word in their writing, otherwise it will not make sense or could give the wrong meaning.
- Revise the homophones *to*, *too* and *two*; *for* and *four*; *there*, *their* and *they're*; and *our* and *are*. (*Our* and *are* are not strictly homophones but in some regions they sound the same or are very similar, and it is useful for the children to be aware of this.)
- Write some sentences on the board that include these words, or ask the children for their suggestions. Decide which spelling is the correct one to use in each case.

Spelling List
- Read the spelling words with the children. Discuss the differences in meaning and spelling between each pair of homophones.
- Point out the silent ‹h› and ‹y› saying /ie/ in *thyme*, the ‹ea› saying /ai/ in *steak*, the silent ‹h› and ‹eir› saying /air/ in *heir*, the ‹eigh› spelling of /ai/ in *weight* and the ‹aa› in *bazaar*.
- Emphasise the pure vowel sounds rather than the schwa (swallowed vowel sound) in *bazaar* and *bizarre* to help the children remember the spelling.
- It is a good idea to blend and sound out the spelling words quickly every day with the children.

die
dye
mail
male
stake
steak
waste
waist
thyme
time
groan
grown
air
heir
wait
weight
bazaar
bizarre

Activity Page
- The children write the meaning for each of the homophones and use a dictionary to check that they are correct. Then they look at the homophone pairs and draw a picture for each word.
- Finally, the children parse the sentence, underlining each part of speech in the correct colour, and identify the subject (*He*). The sentence is written in the simple future and all parts of the verb should be underlined in red. *Ice-cream* is a noun acting as an adjective and should be underlined in blue.

  He will treat Zack to an ice-cream sundae on Sunday.

Dictation
- Provide a sheet of paper for each child and dictate the following sentences:

1. We went on two trips to see the sea.
2. "You have two hundred ewes on the farm," said Tom.
3. Sally asked, "Would you like a walk in the wood?"

Extension Activity
- Write some pairs of homophones on the board: *herd, heard*; *leak, leek*; *write, right*; *pear, pair*; *heal, heel*; *throne, thrown*; *bear, bare*; *sore, soar*; *news, gnus*; *chilli, chilly*; *tow, toe*; *stake, steak*; *red, read*.
- The children draw pictures of the words on a separate sheet of paper. The children should use a dictionary if they are not sure of word meanings.

Grammar: *Identifying Verb Tenses*

Aim
- Reinforce the children's knowledge of the simple and continuous tenses and develop their ability to identify them in sentences (see Verbs, pages 9 to 11).

Introduction
- Write *to help* on the board and ask what sort of word *help* is (a verb). Remind the class that when a verb has *to* in front of it, it is called the infinitive.
- Ask the children which tenses they know (simple past, simple present, simple future, past continuous, present continuous, future continuous) and discuss how they are formed.
- Draw a simple grid of six boxes on the board and write in the tenses as you talk about them:

simple past	simple present	simple future
past continuous	present continuous	future continuous

- Remind the children of the spelling rules for adding the suffixes ‹-ed› and ‹-ing› and how the continuous tenses are formed by using the auxiliary verb *to be* with the present participle.
- Conjugate the irregular verb *to be* with the class in the simple present, past and future, doing the pronoun actions.

Main Point
- Write *I help my dad* on the board and ask which tense the sentence is in (the simple present). Circle the tense in the grid and call out the same sentence in another tense for the children to identify.
- Continue in the same way, using all six tenses:

simple past	simple present	simple future
I helped my dad.	I help my dad.	I shall/will help my dad.
past continuous	present continuous	future continuous
I was helping my dad.	I am helping my dad.	I shall/will be helping my dad.

- Remind the class that the simple present describes an action that is repeated or usual: *I help my dad every day*; while the present continuous describes something that has started and is still happening: *I am helping my dad paint the fence*.
- The simple past describes an action that started and finished within a specific time: *I helped my dad today*; while the continuous past describes an action

that had started and was still happening in the past: *I was helping my dad when the phone rang*.
- Similarly, the simple future describes an action that will start and finish within a specific time: *I shall help my dad tonight*; while the continuous future describes an action that will start and still be happening in the future: *I shall be helping my dad when the race begins*.

Activity Page
- The children write inside the outlined word *Verbs*, using a red pencil. They read each sentence, underlining all parts of the verb in red. They then decide which tense is being used and match it to the correct tense in the tense tents.
- The children then choose a sentence from the previous activity and write it out in the six tenses they know. Finally, they colour the circus poster.

Extension Activity
- Provide a sheet of paper for each child.
- The children choose another sentence from the activity page and write it in the other tenses.

Rounding Off
- Go over the activity page with the children, checking their answers. If they have done the extension activity, ask some of the children to read out their sentences.

Spelling: ‹nch›

Spelling Test
- The children turn to the backs of their books and find the column labelled *Spelling Test 2*.
- In any order, call out the spelling words learnt last week. The children write the words on the lines.

Revision
- Revise the consonant digraphs: ‹ng›, ‹ch›, ‹sh›, ‹th›, ‹qu›; the vowel digraphs: or, oo, ou, oi, er, ar; the five short vowels, /a/, /e/, /i/, /o/, /u/; and the different spellings of the long vowel sounds: /ai/ ‹ai›, ‹ay›, ‹a_e›; /ee/ ‹ee›, ‹ea›, ‹e_e›; /ie/ ‹ie›, ‹y›, ‹igh›, ‹i_e›; /oa/ ‹oa›, ‹ow›, ‹o_e›; /ue/ ‹ue›, ‹ew›, ‹u_e›. Flash cards can be used for reading and sound dictation for spelling.

Spelling Point
- Revise the ‹tch› spelling of the /ch/ sound. This spelling is usually used after a single vowel letter saying a short vowel sound, as in *match*, *fetch*, *itch*, *hopscotch* and *hutch*. Now introduce the spelling pattern ‹nch›. Unlike the ‹t› in ‹tch›, the ‹n› is sounded in ‹nch›. However, as is often the case with consonant blends, children sometimes leave the ‹n› out in their writing because they do not hear it.
- Write some ‹nch› words on the board: *punch*, *bench*, *branch*, *finch* and *poncho*. Blend and sound them out with the class, emphasising the /n/ in ‹nch› each time.

Spelling List
- Read the spelling words with the children, go over the meaning of any words they may not know, and ask them to find and highlight the ‹nch› in each word.
- Point out the ‹qu› in *quench*, that *lunchbox* is a compound word, that ‹ed› says /t/ in *pinched*, the silent ‹w› in *wrench*, the ‹au› spelling in *launch* and *haunches*, the ‹eo› in *luncheon*, and the ‹a› saying /ar/ in *rancher* and *enchantment* (although in some regions this is pronounced /a/, which makes the spelling straightforward).

winch
drench
quench
stench
hunch
lunchbox
scrunch
rancher
flinch
wrench
crunchy
pinched
launch
franchise
luncheon
haunches
henchmen
enchantment

Activity Page
- The children unscramble the letters in the launches and add them to ‹nch› to make words from the spelling list (*drench, quench, winch, rancher, haunches, stench, hunch, wrench, franchise, scrunch, lunchbox, henchmen, pinched, enchantment*). It helps if they cross out each letter as it is used. They then practise writing ‹nch›, first tracing over the dotted

letters before writing along the line with the help of the starting dots.
- Then the children look at the adjective *crunchy* and write its comparative (*crunchier*) and superlative (*crunchiest*) in the elephants. They then unscramble the letters in the anagram (*lunch*) and draw a picture.
- Finally, they parse the sentence, identify the subject (*I*) and choose the correct tense (simple past). *French* is a proper adjective describing the dressing and *my* is a possessive adjective describing who the lunchbox belongs to and both should be underlined in blue.

I drenched the crunchy lettuce in my lunchbox in French dressing.

Dictation
- Provide a sheet of paper for each child and dictate the following sentences:

1. The celery was munchy and crunchy.
2. "Stand in a bunch," ordered the henchman.
3. The witch put an enchantment on the castle.

Extension Activity
- Provide a sheet of paper for each child.
- Write the following anagrams on the board: tuhhc (*hutch*), buhctre (*butcher*), thacw (*watch*), twicsh (*switch*), cbnhe (*bench*). The children unscramble the anagrams and draw a picture for each one.

Grammar: The Subject and Object of a Sentence

Aim
- Refine the children's ability to identify both the subject and object of a sentence. Develop their understanding that all sentences have a subject, but not all sentences have an object.

Introduction
- Briefly revise sentences and phrases. Write *The snake eggs.* on the board and ask whether this is a sentence or a phrase (phrase).
- Ask why it is not a sentence (although it starts with a capital letter, ends in a full stop and makes sense, it has no verb or subject).
- Remind the children that a sentence must make sense, start with a capital letter, contain a subject and verb, and end with a full stop, question mark or exclamation mark.
- If a group of words has no verb but makes sense when you read it, it is usually a phrase.
- Ask the children how the phrase could be turned into a sentence: for example, *The snake eats eggs.* Write it on the board and underline the verb in red.
- Call out some more examples and ask the children whether they are sentences or phrases. When it is a phrase, ask them to turn it into a simple sentence.

Main Point
- Look at the sentence *The snake eats eggs* and remind the children that a sentence must have a subject. The subject is the noun or pronoun that 'does' the verb action; here, it can be identified by asking who, or what, eats eggs.
- Ask the children to identify the subject and draw a box around the word *snake*, with a small ‹s› in the corner.
- Now ask whether the sentence has an object (the noun or pronoun that 'receives' the verb action); the children need to ask themselves *The snake eats what?* to find the answer.
- Draw a ring around *eggs* and put a small ‹o› inside.
- Now replace *eggs* with the pronoun *them* and point out that, like the subject, the object of a sentence is always a noun or pronoun.
- Finally, write *Snake eats.* on the board and discuss how it is a sentence even though it is very short.
- Ask the children whether there is an object (no) and remind them that a sentence always has a subject, but it does not necessarily have an object.

Activity Page
- The children identify the verb in each sentence, underlining all parts of the verb in red (*annoyed, will bake, delivers, arrested, will weigh, dusted, phoned, phoned, carried, sings*).
- They find the subject by deciding who or what is

The Subject and Object of a Sentence

For each sentence, underline the verb in red. Then find the subject and object and write them in their boxes.

subject		object
	Martha annoyed her brother.	brother
	He will bake a cake.	
	A boy delivers the newspapers.	
	The detective arrested the thief.	
	Sanjeev will weigh the flour.	
	Miss Beech dusted the bookshelves.	
	She phoned the doctor.	
	The doctor phoned her.	
	They carried their suitcases upstairs.	
	The little girl sings a happy song.	

Unscramble the anagrams below. All of the words have either ‹nch› or ‹tch› in them.

nrahcb · crhtets · nchum · cubnh · atcmh · chkets

doing the verb action and write it in the rectangular box (*Martha, He, boy, detective, Sanjeev, Miss Beech, She, doctor, They, girl*).
- Then they find the object, deciding who or what is receiving the verb action, and write it in the oval box (*brother, cake, newspapers, thief, flour, bookshelves, doctor, her, suitcases, song*).
- Remind the children to write only the noun or pronoun for the subject and object and not any adjectives or articles that go with it.
- The children then unscramble the anagrams (*branch, stretch, munch, bunch, match, sketch*) and colour the pictures.

Extension Activity
- Provide a sheet of paper for each child.
- The children write some sentences with a subject and an object. Then they work in pairs to identify the subject and object in each others' sentences.

Rounding Off
- Go over the activity page with the children, checking their answers. If they have done the extension activity, ask some of the children to read out their sentences.

Spelling: ‹se› saying /s/

Spelling Test
- The children turn to the backs of their books and find the column labelled *Spelling Test 3*.
- In any order, call out the spelling words learnt last week. The children write the words on the lines.

Revision
- Revise the consonant digraphs: ‹ng›, ‹ch›, ‹sh›, ‹th›, ‹qu›; the vowel digraphs: ‹or›, ‹oo›, ‹ow›, ‹oi›, ‹er›, ‹ar›; the five short vowels, /a/, /e/, /i/, /o/, /u/; and the different spellings of the long vowel sounds: /ai/ ‹ai›, ‹ay›, ‹a_e›; /ee/ ‹ee›, ‹ea›, ‹e_e›; /ie/ ‹ie›, ‹y›, ‹igh›, ‹i_e›; /oa/ ‹oa›, ‹ow›, ‹o_e›; /ue/ ‹ue›, ‹ew›, ‹u_e›. Flash cards can be used for reading and sound dictation for spelling.

Spelling Point
- Revise the main spellings of the /s/ sound that have been taught so far: ‹s› and ‹ce›, ‹ci› and ‹cy› (known as the soft ‹c› spellings).
- Then tell the children that there is another way to write /s/ and this is ‹se›, which usually comes at the end of a word. Write the words *goose* and *geese* on the board and look at how the ‹se› comes at the end of each one. Explain that because the ‹e› is silent, these words have to be learnt for spelling.
- Now write the words *base* and *chase* on the board. Point out that these are not the same as the first two words. The ‹e› in both words is part of the 'hop-over ‹e›' digraph ‹a_e›, and this makes them examples of the ‹s› spelling of /s/.
- Remind the children that ‹se› can sometimes make the /z/ sound, as in *please* and *tease*.

Spelling List
- Read the spelling words with the children, go over the meaning of any words they may not know, and ask them to find and highlight the ‹se› in each word. Point out the ‹ea› spelling of /ee/ in *increase* and *cease*, the compound words *nonsense* and *lighthouse* and the ‹igh› saying /ie/ in *lighthouse*.
- A particularly useful strategy is to 'say it as it sounds', emphasising tricky parts of a word to help the children remember the spelling; for example, it helps to emphasise the pure vowel sound of any schwas (swallowed vowel sounds), as in *reverse*, *collapse* and *nonsense*. It is a good idea to blend and sound out the spelling words quickly every day with the children.

goose
geese
sparse
corpse
dense
horse
increase
promise
reverse
pulse
cease
collapse
immense
disperse
converse
suspense
nonsense
lighthouse

Activity Page
- The children read the phrases and decide which words from the spelling list they describe (*geese, corpse, reverse, lighthouse, cease, increase, converse, sparse, nonsense, collapse, immense, pulse*).
- They then think of words that describe different ways of talking and write them in the speech bubbles (e.g. *shout, yell, yelp, scream, laugh, cry, demand*). Next they think of words that mean *fun* and write them in the web (e.g. *enjoyable, lively, merry, amusing*).
- Finally, they parse the sentence, identify the subject (*crowd*) and choose the correct tense, which is the future continuous. *Horse* is a noun acting as an adjective and should be underlined in blue.

The dense crowd will be dispersing after the horse race.

Dictation
- Dictate the following sentences:

1. The geese were flying north.
2. "The lighthouse looks immense," whispered Sue.
3. Can you reverse the car into the parking space?

Extension Activity
- Provide a sheet of paper for each child.
- The children write down words they could use instead of those in the following list, perhaps using a thesaurus: *glad, wet, red, tired, cold.*

Grammar: Homophones (Your and You're)

Aim
• Refine the children's understanding of homophones and develop their ability to choose between similar-sounding words like *your* and *you're* in their writing.

Introduction
• Revise the possessive adjectives (*my*, *your*, *his/her/its*, *our*, *your*, *their*), which describe who something belongs to. Revise contractions like *don't* and *can't*, where an apostrophe shows that some letters are missing when a pair of words (like *do not*) or one longer word (like *cannot*) is shortened.
• Revise the irregular present tense of the verb *to be* and conjugate it with the children, using the pronoun actions (see Personal Pronouns, page 9).

Main Point
• Remind the children that some words sound similar to one another but have different spellings and meanings. Ask them if they can remember what words like this are called (homophones).
• Ask for suggestions and write them on the board.
• The children have been taught *our* and *are* and *their*, *there* and *they're*, but they may know more.
• Explain that it is very important to use homophones correctly, or written work will not make sense. Before writing a homophone, the children need to decide which meaning is needed and choose the correct spelling.
• Remind the children that the word *our* is a possessive adjective and describes who something belongs to (e.g. *This is our house*), whereas *are* is part of the verb *to be* (e.g. *We are here*). *Our* is more properly pronounced /ou-r/, but in practice it is often pronounced /ar/.
• Remind the children that the word *their* is also a possessive adjective (e.g. *Their house is nearby*), whereas *there* is often used as a pronoun to introduce the subject of a sentence (e.g. *There is our house*), or as an adverb to indicate position (e.g. *The house is over there*). *They're*, however, is a contraction of *they are*: the apostrophe replaces the ‹a› in *are* and joins the two words together. If the children can replace the homophone with *they are* in a sentence and it makes sense, they know to use *they're*.
• Introduce the homophones *your* and *you're*. Write the words on the board and discuss each one. Like *their* and *they're*, one is a possessive adjective and the other is a contraction. Ask the children what they think *you're* is short for (*you are*). Explain that if the homophone in a sentence can be replaced with *you are*, and it makes sense, they should use *you're*.
• Write the following two sentences on the board, leaving a space for *your* and *you're*, and ask the children which word is needed to complete each one:

*You must put on (your) coats to play outside;
(You're) going to play outside today.*
• Ask the children to suggest more sentences using *your* and *you're*, write them on the board and discuss which word is needed in each one.

Activity Page
• The children write inside the outlined words at the top of the sheet and practise writing the words on the lines. Then they read the sentences, decide which words complete the sentences (*You're, your, you're, your*) and cross out the incorrect answers.
• Next, the children write inside the outlined words in the middle of the sheet.
• Lastly, they read the sentences at the bottom of the sheet, decide which word(s) are needed to complete each one and write them in (*there, your, our, You're, Are, you're, their, their, there, they're*).

Extension Activity
• Working in pairs, the children take it in turns to dictate and write sentences that contain *your* and *you're*. They then work out whether they have used the correct spellings.

Rounding Off
• Go over the children's work, checking their answers. If they have done the extension activity, ask some of the children to read out their sentences.

Spelling: ‹ve› saying /v/

Spelling Test
- The children turn to the backs of their books and find the column labelled *Spelling Test 4*.
- In any order, call out the spelling words learnt last week. The children write the words on the lines.

Revision
- Revise the consonant digraphs: ‹ng›, ‹ch›, ‹sh›, ‹th›, ‹qu›; the vowel digraphs: ‹or›, ‹oo›, ‹ou›, ‹oi›, ‹er›, ‹ar›; the five short vowels, /a/, /e/, /i/, /o/, /u/; and the different spellings of the long vowel sounds: /ai/ ‹ai›, ‹ay›, ‹a_e›; /ee/ ‹ee›, ‹ea›, ‹e_e›; /ie/ ‹ie›, ‹y›, ‹igh›, ‹i_e›; /oa/ ‹oa›, ‹ow›, ‹o_e›; /ue/ ‹ue›, ‹ew›, ‹u_e›. Flash cards can be used for reading and sound dictation for spelling.

Spelling Point
- Revise the ‹se› spelling of the /s/ sound and the ‹v› spelling of the /v/ sound. Explain that, like the ‹se› spelling of /s/, /v/ can also be spelt ‹ve› and it also usually comes at the end of a word.
- Write the words *twelve* and *solve* on the board and point out that the ‹ve› comes at the end of each one.
- Explain that English words rarely end in the letter ‹v›, so if the /v/ sound comes at the end of a word, the spelling is likely to be ‹ve›.
- Now write the words *dive* and *hive* on the board. Point out that these are not the same as the first two words. The ‹e› in both words is part of the 'hop-over ‹e›' digraph ‹i_e›, and this makes them examples of the ‹v› spelling of /v/.

Spelling List
- Read the spelling words with the children, go over the meaning of any words they may not know, and ask them to find and highlight the ‹ve› in each word.
- Point out the ‹ur› spelling of /er/ in *curve*, the ‹s› saying /z/ in *deserve*, *eavesdrop*, *dissolve* and *observe*, the ‹au› saying /oa/ in *mauve*, the ‹ea› saying /ee/ in *eavesdrop* and *bereavement* and the ‹ie› saying /ee/ in *retrieve*. It can also help to remember certain spellings to 'say it as it sounds'.
- It is a good idea to blend and sound out the spelling words quickly every day with the children.

twelve
nerve
solve
carve
starve
groove
curve
deserve
evolve
involve
conserve
mauve
eavesdrop
dissolve
observe
retrieve
revolve
bereavement

Activity Page
- The children write in the spelling word that completes each sentence (*curve, solve, eavesdrop, retrieve, observe, twelve, dissolve, deserve, starve,*

involve, mauve, carve). They then add the correct punctuation to the sentences (1. *"Are we going through the revolving door?" asked Gran.* 2. *I bought apples, bananas, pears and oranges.* 3. *"I have a new book," said Zack proudly.* 4. *"What a nerve!" exclaimed Fred.* 5. *Do they deserve to win the game?*).
- Finally, they parse the sentence, underlining each part of speech in the correct colour, identify the subject (*bird*) and choose the correct tense, which is the past continuous, so all parts of the verb should be underlined in red. *Conservation* is a noun acting as an adjective and should be underlined in blue.
  The rare bird was nesting quietly in the conservation area.

Dictation
- Provide a sheet of paper for each child and dictate the following sentences:

1. The waiter is serving twelve people.
2. The chef carves the joint of beef.
3. They solved the clues for the crossword.

Extension Activity
- Write some more sentences on the board, leaving boxes where punctuation marks should be.
- The children write down the sentences, adding in the correct punctuation.

Grammar: Antonyms

Aim
• Develop the children's understanding of opposites, which are words with the opposite meaning to other words. Introduce the term *antonym*.

Introduction
• Briefly revise thesauruses and how they list words with similar meanings. Finding alternative words in a thesaurus can help make sentences more interesting and avoid overusing certain words.
• Explain that thesauruses also list words with the opposite meaning to the word you are looking up.
• Ask the children if they can remember what these words are called (opposites or antonyms). Make sure the children know that opposites are also called antonyms.
• Now revise prefixes and suffixes; these are one or more syllables added to a word to change its meaning. Prefixes are added at the beginning of a word and suffixes come at the end.
• Write some examples on the board. Explain that many prefixes and some suffixes can be used to create antonyms: ‹un-›, ‹im-› and ‹non-› mean *not*; ‹de-› and ‹dis-› mean *undo* or *remove*; ‹mis-› means *wrongly* or *not*; ‹ex-› means *out* or *away from*; and ‹-less› and ‹-ful› make adjectives with the opposite meaning, either *without* something or *full* of it.

Main Point
• Call out these words and ask the children for their antonyms: *day* (*night*), *hot* (*cold*), *quiet* (*noisy*), *up* (*down*), *hard* (*soft*), *asleep* (*awake*), *right* (*left*).
• Point out that sometimes there is an obvious antonym like *night* for *day* and *down* for *up*.
• Prefixes and suffixes often create opposites. Ask the children which prefix could be used to make the opposite of *possible* (**im**possible), *appear* (**dis**appear) and *comfortable* (**un**comfortable), and which suffix could be used instead of ‹-ful› to make the opposite of *painful* (*pain**less***).
• Sometimes a word has more than one antonym: for example, *loud* and *noisy* are both antonyms for *quiet*.
• Write on the board, *The aquarium has a big fish*. Ask the class to suggest an antonym to give an opposite description of *big*. Write their suggestions on the board: possible examples are *small*, *tiny*, *little* and *minute*. Point out that all these words could be put in a 'word web' as they have similar meanings.
• However, sometimes a word has more than one antonym, but the meanings are not the same. For example, *wrong* and *left* are both antonyms for *right*. Similarly, *easy* is an antonym for *hard* but it does not mean the same as *soft*. Remind the children that sometimes a word can

have several meanings and that different meanings will have different antonyms.

Activity Page
• The children write antonyms for the words in the mirrors (*achieve: fail, mythical: real, singular: plural, husbands: wives, private: public, cheerless: cheerful*).
• They then rewrite each sentence, replacing the word in bold with an antonym (*entrance, increase, false, male, husband's*). In both of these exercises there is sometimes more than one possible answer, but as long as it makes sense, it is correct.
• Next, the children write as many antonyms as they can think of for the word *big*.
• Finally, they add the correct punctuation to the sentences.

Extension Activity
• Write these sentences on the board: *My jacket is too tight; It was a sharp pencil. The people were very friendly. My bedroom is always tidy. The experiment was a failure. The dog was barking outside. She quietly opened the door.*
• The children rewrite each sentence, replacing the underlined word with an antonym.

Rounding Off
• Go over the children's work, checking their answers.

Spelling: Plurals ‹ves›

Spelling Test
- The children turn to the backs of their books and find the column labelled *Spelling Test 5*.
- In any order, call out the spelling words learnt last week. The children write the words on the lines.

Revision
- Revise the consonant digraphs: ‹ng›, ‹ch›, ‹sh›, ‹th›, ‹qu›; the vowel digraphs: ‹or›, ‹oo›, ‹ou›, ‹oi›, ‹er›, ‹ar›; the five vowel short vowels, /a/, /e/, /i/, /o/, /u/; and the different spellings of the long vowel sounds: /ai/ ‹ai›, ‹ay›, ‹a_e›; /ee/ ‹ee›, ‹ea›, ‹e_e›; /ie/ ‹ie›, ‹y›, ‹igh›, ‹i_e›; /oa/ ‹oa›, ‹ow›, ‹o_e›; /ue/ ‹ue›, ‹ew›, ‹u_e›. Flash cards can be used for reading and sound dictation for spelling.

Spelling Point
- Revise the ‹ve› spelling of the /v/ sound. Remind the children that it usually comes at the end of a word.
- Now write *scarves* and *wives* on the board and ask the children what they notice about these two words. They should be able to point out that the /v/ sound is written ‹ve› but they may also notice that ‹ve› does not come right at the end of either word, but in both cases it is followed by ‹s›.
- Ask the children why this is (they are plural nouns) and then ask them to call out the singular for each word (*scarf*, *wife*).
- Explain that some singular words ending in ‹f› have an irregular plural made by removing the ‹f› and adding the suffix ‹-ves›, as in *scarves*. If the word ends in a 'hop-over ‹e›' digraph, as in *wife*, the plural is made by replacing the ‹fe› with ‹ves›. Not all singular nouns ending in ‹f› or ‹fe› make their plurals in this way, so the spellings have to be learnt.

Spelling List
- Read the spelling words with the children, go over the meaning of any words they may not know, and ask them to find and highlight the ‹ves› in each word
- Point out that *lives*, the plural of *life* is said with an /ie/, unlike the verb *lives*, which has the /i/ sound
- Also point out the ‹ea› spelling of /ee/ in *leaves*, the silent ‹k› and ‹h› in *knives* and *wharves*, the /o/ saying /oo/ in *wolves*, the ‹a› in *halves* and *calves*, the ‹ie› saying /ee/ in *thieves* and the ‹ar› saying /or/ in *wharves* and *dwarves*.
- Also make sure the children know the difference in meaning and spelling between the plural *calves* and the verb *carves* from last week's spelling list.

Spelling List words:
scarves
selves
wives
lives
elves
loaves
hooves
leaves
knives
wolves
shelves
halves
calves
thieves
wharves
dwarves
ourselves
themselves

Plurals: ‹ves›

Make these plural words from the spelling list into singular nouns.

scarves, selves, wives, lives, elves, loaves, hooves, leaves, knives, wolves, shelves, halves, calves, thieves, wharves, dwarves, ourselves, themselves

selves _____ knives _____
scarves _____ wolves _____
wives _____ shelves _____
elves _____ halves _____
lives _____ calves _____
loaves _____ thieves _____
hooves _____ wharves _____
leaves _____ dwarves _____

Write the plural of each noun and draw some more examples so that the pictures match the words.

monkey _____
radio _____
goose _____
tomato _____
bush _____
cherry _____

Parse this sentence, identify the subject and choose the correct tense.

The greedy thieves are stealing the warm loaves from the bakery shelves.

12

Activity Page
- The children write the singular for each of the plurals (*self, scarf, wife, elf, life, loaf, hoof, leaf, knife, wolf, shelf, half, calf, thief, wharf, dwarf*). They then write the correct plural for each noun (*monkeys, geese, radios, bushes, tomatoes, cherries*).
- Finally, they parse the sentence, identify the subject (*thieves*) and choose the correct tense, which is the present continuous, so all parts of the verb should be underlined in red. *Bakery* is a noun acting as an adjective and should be underlined in blue.

The greedy thieves are stealing the warm loaves from the bakery shelves.

Dictation
- Dictate the following sentences:

1. The baker put the loaves on the shelves.
2. The cows and their calves grazed in the field.
3. "Are the knives sharp?" asked the butcher.

Extension Activity
- Provide a sheet of paper for each child.
- Write these nouns on the board: *bat, brush, daisy, box, foot, fly, car, pencil, man*.
- The children write the plurals (*bats, brushes, daisies, boxes, feet, flies, cars, pencils, men*) and then draw a picture for each one, drawing more than one of each item to show that the word is plural.

Grammar: *Plural Nouns in Sentences*

Aim
- Introduce the idea that if a singular noun in a sentence is made plural, the rest of the sentence must agree.

Introduction
- A regular plural is usually made by adding a suffix to a singular noun. Revise these terms with the class, discuss the different suffixes that can be used and revise any the children are unsure of:
- The most common suffix for a plural is ‹-s› (e.g. *dog, dogs; house, houses; car, cars*).
- If a noun ends in ‹ch›, ‹sh›, ‹s›, ‹z› or ‹x›, add ‹-es› (e.g. *watches, bushes, glasses, boxes*).
- If a noun ends in ‹o›, add ‹-es› (e.g. *tomatoes, potatoes, tornadoes*). But if the words are foreign, abbreviations or have a vowel before the ‹o›, add ‹-s› (e.g. *pianos, kilos, studios*).
- If a noun ends in a vowel + ‹y›, add ‹-s› (e.g. *boys, days, keys*).
- If a noun ends in a consonant + ‹y›, replace ‹y› with 'shy ‹i›' and add ‹-es› (e.g. *cherries, flies*).
- Irregular, or 'tricky', plurals are not made in this way and have to be learnt. Discuss the plural ‹ves› spelling for some singular words ending in ‹f› or ‹fe› (see page 42). Ask the children for other irregular plurals and discuss what makes them tricky. Some animals are the same in the singular or plural, as in *sheep, deer, fish, moose* and *salmon*. Others change the vowel sound, as in *foot* and *feet, mouse* and *mice*, while others like *children* and *people* are very different to their singular nouns *child* and *person*.

Main Point
- Write *The dog chews the bone* on the board and ask what the plural of *bone* is. Add ‹s› to make *bones* and read the sentence again; the rest of the words stay the same even though the noun *bone* is now plural.
- Now tell the class that you are going to see what happens if the indefinite article, *a*, is used instead of the definite article, *the*. Write *The dog chews a bone*, change *bone* to *bones* and read out the sentence, *The dog chews a bones*. Ask what is wrong with the sentence and discuss how it can be put right.
- Explain that if you make a noun in a sentence plural, the other words connected to it must still make sense, or agree. *The* can be used with singular and plural nouns, which is why only the plural changed in the first sentence, whereas *a* shows that there is only one of the noun so is never used with a plural.
- Discuss what could be used instead of *a* to go with *bones* (e.g. *the, some, many, two, a lot of, a few*). Put them into the sentence to see if they make sense.
- Now ask what happens if the other noun, *dog*, is made plural. Write *The dogs chews the bones* and ask why

this sounds wrong. Explain that *dogs* is the subject of the sentence, and the verb and subject must always agree, so it should be *The dogs **chew** the bones*.

Activity Page
- The children write inside the outlined word *Nouns*, using a black pencil.
- They then rewrite each sentence so that the singular noun(s) in bold become plural (*sunflowers, dresses, prizes, donkeys, fields, berries, bushes, men, trees, fiddles, flutes, drums*), checking that the rest of the sentence still makes sense. None of the nouns are the subject of the sentence so the children do not have to worry about making the verb agree. However, they must replace *a* with something that agrees with the plural. Finally, the children draw pictures to illustrate the sentences.

Extension Activity
- Write the sentences on the board: *The policeman chased a thief. "Come and play," said the boy. I had a sandwich at lunchtime. She picked a strawberry in the garden.* The children rewrite the sentences so that the underlined nouns become plural and everything agrees (*thieves, boys, sandwiches, strawberries*).
- They then draw pictures to match the sentences.

Rounding Off
- Go over the children's work, checking their answers.

Plural Nouns in Sentences — Nouns

Rewrite each sentence so that any nouns in bold are plural. Make sure that the sentence still makes sense and change any other words where necessary. Draw several pictures of each item to match.

- I grew a **sunflower** in a big pot.
- Beth tried on the new **dress**.
- Jenny won a **prize** in the competition.
- He keeps a **donkey** in the **field**.
- The bird ate a **berry** from the **bush**.
- The lion chased the **man** up a **tree**.
- The band had a **fiddle**, **flute** and **drum**.

Spelling: Schwa ‹a›

Spelling Test
- The children turn to the backs of their books and find the column labelled *Spelling Test 6*.
- Call out the spelling words learnt last week.

Revision
- Revise syllables and how to identify them in words by clapping the syllables or doing 'chin bumps' (see Syllables, pages 22 to 23). Remind the children that the number of vowel sounds in a word is the same as the number of syllables. Write these words on the board: *arch/way, bash/ful, rock/et, en/chant/ment*. Underline the letters making the vowel sounds and separate the words into syllables.

Spelling Point
- Write the word *doc/tor* on the board and ask the children how many syllables it has (two). Identify the vowel sounds and split the word into two syllables with a line. Explain that if a word has two or more syllables, we put a stress on one of them: that is, we say it slightly louder, to give it more emphasis.
- Ask the children which syllable is stressed in *doctor* (the first syllable) and then see if they can hear the stressed syllable in other words. Point out that in a stressed syllable, you will hear the vowel sound clearly in its pure form, such as the /o/ in *doctor*.
- However, sometimes the vowel in an unstressed syllable gets swallowed and sounds more like an /uh/ sound. This swallowed vowel sound is called a schwa and is the most common vowel sound in English. This is why it helps to remember the spelling by 'saying it as it sounds', saying the schwa in its pure form, as in 'doct-or' rather than 'doct-uh'.

Spelling List
- Read the spelling words with the children and ask them to find and highlight any ‹a› saying the schwa in each word. For words with more than one ‹a›, the schwa is shown here in bold: *pasta, banana, panda, anagram, harass* or *harass* (depending on where the stress is put), *magazine, embarrass, exclamation, paragraph, guarantee, abominable*.
- Point out the 'hop-over ‹e›' digraph ‹i_e› saying /ee/ in *magazine*, the soft ‹c› in *entrance* and *announcement*, the suffixes in *exclamation*, *abominable* and *announcement*, the ‹ph› saying /f/ in *paragraph*, and the silent ‹u› in *guarantee*.

pasta
avoid
banana
panda
comma
hexagon
anagram
husband
harass
private
magazine
embarrass
exclamation
paragraph
guarantee
entrance
abominable
announcement

Activity Page
- The children identify the syllables in the words (*hex/a/gon, ba/na/na, com/ma, pan/da, pas/ta, a/void, har/ass, pri/vate, hus/band, mag/a/zine, em/bar/rass, an/a/gram, a/bom/i/na/ble, en/trance, ex/cla/ma/tion, par/a/graph, guar/an/tee, an/nounce/ment*).
- They then unscramble the anagrams (*pasta, anchovy, loaves, cheese, banana, steak, potato, cucumber*).
- The children then write two lists, using a comma to separate each item (except for the last two items, which should be separated by *and*). Finally, they parse the sentence, identify the subject (*pirate*) and choose the correct tense (simple past). *Successfully* is an adverb made by adding ‹-ly› to the adjective *successful* and should be underlined in orange.
  The abominable pirate successfully avoided the hurricane.

Dictation
- Dictate the following sentences:

1. A panda is a black and white animal.
2. I am writing a paragraph about the magazine.
3. A hexagon is a shape with six sides.

Extension Activity
- The children practise using commas by writing another sentence that includes a list.

Grammar: Synonyms

Aim
- Develop the children's ability to choose interesting words in their writing, and introduce the term *synonym*.

Introduction
- Briefly revise opposites and make sure the children understand the term *antonym*.
- Remind them that many prefixes and some suffixes can be used to make antonyms.
- Call out some words and ask the class to suggest an antonym for each one: *true* (*false*), *black* (*white*), *tall* (*short*), *shallow* (*deep*), *last* (*first*), *empty* (*full*), *end* (*beginning*), *new* (*old*), *impossible* (*possible*), *careless* (*careful*), *untie* (*tie*).
- Also point out that some words can have several antonyms: for example, antonyms for *happy* include *unhappy*, *sad*, *glum* and *gloomy*. Sometimes a word can have more than one meaning and each meaning will have different antonyms: antonyms for *right* are *left* (as in direction) and *wrong* (as in correctness).
- Remind the children that a thesaurus will help them find antonyms for a word.

Main Point
- Now ask the children, *What is the opposite of opposite?* If you look up *opposite* in a thesaurus, its antonym is *same*.
- Remind the class that a thesaurus also lists words with the same or similar meanings. These words have a special name too: they are called synonyms, and they are the words that are used in word webs.
- Finding alternative words can help make sentences more interesting or add extra meaning.
- Ask the children if they can remember any of the synonyms they wrote for *converse* on page 8 of their *Pupil Books* (see page 38). Try putting one of those words into a sentence and then replace it with another. Discuss what effect this has on the sentence.
- Now write *I saw a big spider* on the board and underline the word *big*. Ask the class to suggest words that could be used instead of *big* and write them on the board.
- Synonyms for *big* include: *large, huge, great, giant, gigantic, enormous, massive, mighty, immense, mammoth, colossal, vast, tall, high, lofty, towering, powerful, bulky, heavy, hefty, weighty, sturdy, important, significant, major*.

Activity Page
- The children think of as many synonyms as they can for the word *big* and write them in the word web.

- They then rewrite the sentences, replacing *big* with a different synonym each time.
- Finally, the children write two lists, using a comma to separate each item (except for the last two items, which should be separated by *and*).

Extension Activity
- Provide a sheet of paper for each child.
- Write the following words on the board: *rough, funny, clever, honest, kind, strong, weak, confused, change, wet, make, jump, loud, run, thin, wide, elegant, shiny, clean, dirty, unwell, dangerous, careless, boring.*
- Each child picks a word, draws a word web and fills it with as many synonyms for their word as possible. They can use a thesaurus to help add to the list.
- Alternatively, the children could help create a large word web for *big* to be used in the classroom.

Rounding Off
- Go over the activity page with the children, checking their answers.
- If they have done the extension activity, ask some of the children to read out their synonyms.

Spelling: Schwa ‹o›

Spelling Test
- The children turn to the backs of their books and find the column labelled *Spelling Test 7*.
- Call out the spelling words learnt last week.

Revision
- Revise syllables and how to identify them in words by clapping the syllables or doing 'chin bumps' (see Syllables, pages 22 to 23). Remind the children that the number of vowel sounds in a word is the same as the number of syllables.
- Write these words on the board: *a*/*void*, *pan*/*da*, *com*/*ma*, *pas*/*ta*. With the class, identify the vowel sounds, underline the letters making them, separate the words into syllables, and decide which one is stressed.

Spelling Point
- Revise the schwa and remind the children that this swallowed vowel sound is the most common vowel sound in English. Also remind them that the schwa only appears in unstressed syllables.
- Write the word *lem*/*on* on the board and ask the children how many syllables it has (two). Identify the vowel sounds with the class and split the word into two syllables with a line. Say the word with the class, clapping once for each syllable.
- Ask the children which syllable is stressed in *lemon* (the first syllable). Point out that the pure /e/ can be heard in the stressed syllable, whereas the ‹o› in the unstressed syllable sounds more like an /uh/ sound and is therefore a schwa. Explain that the schwa sound in an unstressed syllable can be made by any of the vowels and this is one of the reasons why English words can be tricky to spell.

Spelling List
- Read the spelling words with the children and go over the meaning of any words they may not know.
- Ask them to find and highlight any ‹o› saying the schwa in each word (for words with more than one ‹o›, the schwa is shown here in bold: *coc**o**nut, opp**o**site, croc**o**dile, apostr**o**phe, apol**o**gy, c**o**njunction, hom**o**phone*). Clap the syllables in each word and see if the children can hear where the stress is.
- Point out the ‹se› saying /s/ in *purpose*, the silent ‹d› in *handsome*, the ‹i_e› saying /i/ in *opposite*, the ‹y› and ‹e› saying /ee/ on the end of *absolutely*, *apostrophe* and *apology*, the ‹ph›

lemon
carrot
agony
coconut
second
purpose
handsome
opposite
button
violin
method
crocodile
absolutely
apostrophe
recognise
apology
conjunction
homophone

saying /f/ in *apostrophe* and *homophone*, the ‹s› saying /z/ in *recognise* and the suffix in *conjunc**tion***.

Activity Page
- The children put the jumbled syllables into the correct order to make the spelling words (*carrot, purpose, coconut, agony, lemon, second, handsome, method, button, crocodile, violin, opposite, homophone, apology, conjunction, recognise, apostrophe, absolutely*).
- They then complete the sentences by writing the correct spelling of the missing homophones (*You're, your; Your, you're; You're, your; there, their; They're; to; to, too; two*).
- Then, they match the homophones (*pair, pear; our, are; flower, flour*).
- Finally, they parse the sentence, identify the subject (*She*) and choose the correct tense (future continuous). *Lemon, coconut* and *carrot* are nouns acting as adjectives and should be underlined in blue. She will be using a new method for the lemon, coconut and carrot cakes.

Dictation
- Dictate the following sentences:

1. The second button on his coat was missing.
2. We chopped carrots and potatoes for the stew.
3. The handsome pirate apologised for his awful deed.

Grammar: Concrete Nouns

Aim
- Refine the children's knowledge of nouns, and introduce the term *concrete noun*. Concrete nouns are common nouns that you can see, hear, smell, taste or touch.

Introduction
- Revise nouns. Nouns are the names given to particular people, places and dates (proper nouns) or things (common nouns). The colour for the all types of noun is black.
- Remind the children that proper nouns start with a capital letter.
- Revise the actions: for proper nouns the children touch their foreheads with their index and middle fingers; for common nouns they touch their foreheads with one hand.
- Remind the children that the words *a* or *an* (the indefinite articles) and *the* (the definite article) can usually be put in front of a common noun. For example, *On <u>Monday</u>, <u>Jane</u> and <u>Zack</u> saw **a** <u>bird</u> sitting on **an** <u>egg</u> in the <u>nest</u>.*
- Write some sentences on the board, identify the proper nouns and common nouns, and underline them in black.

Main Point
- There are three types of common noun: concrete, abstract and collective. So far the children have learnt to think about common nouns as things they can see and touch (these are concrete nouns, but the children will not be familiar with this term yet), or as the name for a group of people, animals or things, such as *a **class** of children* or *a **herd** of cows* (collective nouns).
- Explain that the common nouns that we can see and touch are called concrete nouns; they are concrete because they have a physical form that can be experienced through one or more of the five senses.
- Discuss what is meant by the five senses and write them on the board. Ask the children to call out some concrete nouns for each sense. Discuss which of the other senses they can be experienced by too.

> Sight: *tree, floor, chair, shoe, bed*
> Hearing: *bell, telephone, radio, bird, frog*
> Smell: *smoke, perfume, rose, coffee, paint*
> Taste: *sugar, vinegar, milk, mint, salt*
> Touch: *silk, water, wool, ice, sand*

- Call out some proper nouns and some concrete nouns. After each word, the children decide which type of noun it is and do the appropriate action.

Activity Page
- The children the think of as many concrete nouns as they can for each of the five senses and write them in the appropriate concrete blocks.

Extension Activity
- The children can make a concrete noun wall for the classroom.
- Cut out rectangles of grey paper in different sizes to represent concrete blocks. Ask the children to write a different concrete noun on each one.
- They could do it in a graffiti style with bold colours and bubble or angular writing, and draw pictures to illustrate the nouns.

Rounding Off
- Go over the activity page with the children, checking their answers.

Spelling: Schwa ‹u›

Spelling Test
- The children turn to the backs of their books and find the column labelled *Spelling Test 8*.
- Call out the spelling words learnt last week.

Revision
- Revise syllables and how to identify them in words by clapping the syllables or doing 'chin bumps' (see Syllables, pages 22 to 23).
- Remind the children that the number of vowel sounds in a word is the same as the number of syllables.
- Write these words on the board: *lem/on, but/ton, pur/pose, sec/ond*. With the class, identify the vowel sounds, underline the letters making them, separate the words into syllables, and decide which one is stressed.

Spelling Point
- Revise the schwa, which is a swallowed vowel sound that often appears in unstressed syllables. Remind the children that the schwa is the most common vowel sound in English and it can be the sound of any swallowed vowel.
- Write the word *cac/tus* on the board and ask the children how many syllables it has (two). Identify the vowel sounds and split the word into two syllables with a line. Say the word with the class, clapping once for each syllable. Ask the children which syllable is stressed in *cactus* (the first syllable). Point out that the pure /a/ can be heard in the stressed syllable, whereas the ‹u› in the unstressed syllable sounds more like an /uh/ sound and is therefore a schwa.

Spelling List
- Read the spelling words with the children. Ask them to find and highlight any ‹u› saying the schwa in each word (for words with more than one ‹u›, the schwa is shown here in bold: *fungus, beautiful, thesaurus*). Clap syllables in each word and see if the children can hear where the stress is.
- Draw attention to how the 'magic' in a vowel can change the preceding short vowel sound into a long one, as in *virus, focus, minus, medium* and *genius*.
- Point out the ‹n› in *fungus* saying /ng/ (as the /g/ is spoken), the suffix ‹-ful› in *careful* and *beautiful*, the soft ‹c› and ‹g› in *success* and *genius*, the ‹eer› saying /ear/ in *volunteer*, the ‹eau› saying

fungus
cactus
virus
focus
minus
album
medium
careful
difficult
success
genius
volunteer
maximum
minimum
beautiful
thesaurus
instrument
hippopotamus

/ue/ in *beautiful* and the ‹au› spelling in *thesaurus*.
- It is a good idea to blend and sound out the spelling words quickly every day with the children.

Activity Page
- The children find the spelling words in the word search and work out which one is missing (*instrument*).
- Then they think of synonyms for the words in the webs and write them in the spaces. The children can use a thesaurus to help them if they have one.
- Finally, they parse the sentence, identify the subject (*musician*) and choose the correct tense (simple present). *Her* and *its* are possessive adjectives, which describe who or what the instrument and the case belong to, and should be underlined in blue. *Beautiful* is an adjective made by adding the suffix ‹-ful› to the noun *beauty*. *Carefully* is an adverb made by adding the suffix ‹-ly› to the adjective *careful* and should be underlined in orange.

The musician carefully places her beautiful instrument inside its case.

Dictation
- Dictate the following sentences:

1. A cactus is a plant that grows in the desert.
2. Is the violin a difficult instrument to play?
3. I saw a crocodile, a panda and a hippopotamus.

Grammar: Abstract Nouns

Aim
- Refine the children's knowledge of nouns, and introduce the concept of abstract nouns.
- Abstract nouns are the names for things like ideas, feelings, actions, qualities and events.

Introduction
- Revise proper nouns and common nouns. Nouns are the names given to particular people, places and dates (proper nouns, starting with a capital letter) or things (common nouns, often with *a*, *an* or *the* in front). The colour for all types of noun is black.
- Revise the actions: for proper nouns the children touch their foreheads with their index and middle fingers; for common nouns they touch their foreheads with their hands.
- Ask the children what kind of common nouns they know. So far they have learnt about collective nouns, which are the names for groups of people, animals or things (e.g. a *bunch of bananas* or a *band of musicians*), and concrete nouns, which are things we can see, hear, smell, taste or touch.
- Ask some children to say a concrete noun and do the action, gently tapping their forehead twice with their hand. Write the examples on the board and discuss which of the senses experience them.

Main Point
- Ask whether any of the children know the word *abstract* and what it means. If something is abstract, it exists in thought or as an idea, but is not a physical thing.
- Show the children a picture of an abstract painting. Discuss how it is made up of shapes and patterns rather than realistic depictions of people or objects. Explain that abstract art is meant to express an idea or emotion. Ask the children how the painting makes them feel.
- Explain that not all common nouns have a physical or *concrete* form that can be experienced through the five senses.
- Write two phrases on the board: *the boy's <u>dog</u>*; *the boy's <u>love</u> for his dog*. Underline *dog* and *love*. *Dog* and *love* are both nouns belonging to the boy. However, while you can see, hear, smell and touch a dog, you cannot experience love in this way: love is an emotion, not an object. Therefore, it is an abstract noun.
- Explain that abstract nouns are the names for ideas, feelings, actions, qualities and events.
- Think of some more examples and discuss them with the class (e.g. *happiness, sadness, anger, amazement, anxiety, delight, envy, excitement, fear, hope, surprise, worry, beauty, kindness, bravery, confidence, fairness, talent, intelligence, weakness,*

peace, war, freedom, taste, knowledge, romance, hate, government, ideas, time, adventure, weather).
- Call out some proper nouns, concrete nouns and abstract nouns and ask the children to do the appropriate action for each one.

Activity Page
- The children write inside the outlined abstract nouns in the thought bubbles with a black pencil.
- They then complete each sentence with one of the five abstract nouns (*time, pain, tide, shock, adventure*). Finally, the children sort the words at the bottom of the page into proper, concrete and abstract nouns, writing them in the three columns.

Extension Activity
- Ask the children to draw a grid like that at the bottom of the activity page.
- Write the following words on the board: *Anna, apple, bravery, trumpet, Europe, car, experience, January, illness, Monday, lamp, jealousy, power, lion, Australia, Chicago, happiness, dress.*
- The children sort the words into proper, concrete and abstract nouns and write them into the grid.
- The children could also make abstract noun clouds to display in the classroom.

Rounding Off
- Go over the activity page with the children.

Spelling: Schwa ‹ar›

Spelling Test
- The children turn to the backs of their books and find the column labelled *Spelling Test 9*.
- Call out the spelling words learnt last week.

Revision
- Revise syllables and how to identify them in words by clapping the syllables or doing 'chin bumps'. Remind the children that the number of vowel sounds in a word is the same as the number of syllables.
- Write these words on the board: *cac/tus, vi/rus, mi/nus, al/bum*. With the class, identify the vowel sounds, underline the letters making them, separate the words into syllables, and decide which one is stressed.
- Point out that the first syllable in *virus* and *minus* ends in ‹i› saying its long vowel sound: this is called an open syllable. Each of the second syllables has a short vowel sound followed by a consonant: this is called a closed syllable.

Spelling Point
- Revise the schwa, which is a swallowed vowel sound that often appears in unstressed syllables. Remind the children that the schwa is the most common vowel sound in English and because it can be the sound of any swallowed vowel, this makes spelling words with a schwa tricky.
- Write the word *dol/lar* on the board and ask the children how many syllables it has (two). Identify the vowel sounds with the class and split the word into two syllables with a line. Say the word with the class, clapping once for each syllable. Ask the children which syllable is stressed in *dollar* (the first). Point out that the pure /o/ can be heard in the stressed syllable, whereas the ‹ar› in the unstressed syllable sounds more like an /uh/ sound and is therefore a schwa.

Spelling List
- Read the spelling words with the children and ask them to find and highlight the ‹ar› saying the schwa in each word. Clap the syllables in each word and see if the children can hear where the stress is.
- Point out the soft ‹c› in *cellar*, the ‹su› saying /shoo/ in *sugar*, the 'magic' in the schwa making the ‹u› say its long vowel sound /ue/ in *popular, regular, particular* and *spectacular*, and the alternative spellings ‹ur› and ‹ow› in *burglar* and *coward*.

grammar
custard
cellar
sugar
wizard
dollar
popular
coward
burglar
regular
orchard
forward
standard
separate
calendar
familiar
particular
spectacular

Schwa ‹ar›

grammar
custard
cellar
sugar
wizard
dollar

popular
coward
burglar
regular
orchard
forward

standard
separate
calendar
familiar
particular
spectacular

leaves
scarves
geese
thieves

The words from the spelling list have been misspelt. Correct each one, using a different colour, and then write it correctly underneath.

gramer ✗ — wizerd ✗ — bergler ✗
populer ✗ — shuger ✗ — sellar ✗
kusterd ✗ — foreword ✗ — reguelar ✗
oarchard ✗ — calander ✗ — doller ✗
famillyar ✗ — standerd ✗ — seperait ✗
partikuler ✗ — specacuelar ✗ — kowerd ✗

Write out the singular noun for each of these plural words.

parents ___ — dollars ___
spiders ___ — anchovies ___
foxes ___ — deer ___
pirates ___ — viruses ___
pianos ___ — mice ___
babies ___ — apologies ___

Parse this sentence, identify the subject and choose the correct tense.
The cowardly burglar is hiding in the castle's cellar.

simple past | simple present | simple future
past continuous | present continuous | future continuous

20

Activity Page
- The children look at the misspelt words from the spelling list and write the correct spellings underneath. They then write the singular noun for each of the plurals (*parent, dollar, spider, anchovy, leaf, fox, deer, scarf, pirate, virus, goose, piano, mouse, thief, baby, apology*).
- Finally, they parse the sentence, identify the subject (*burglar*) and choose the correct tense (present continuous). Adverbs often end in ‹-ly›, but *cowardly* is an adjective describing the burglar. *Castle's* is a possessive noun, which acts as an adjective.
  The cowardly burglar is hiding in the castle's cellar.

Dictation
- Dictate the following sentences:

1. Apple pie and custard is a popular dish.
2. It was an ordinary Saturday afternoon.
3. The burglar stole two thousand American dollars.

Extension Activity
- Write these nouns on the board: *paragraph, radish, sheep, crocodile, knife, agony, lunchbox, success, woman, half, coconut, magazine*. The children write the plural for each one (*paragraphs, radishes, sheep, crocodiles, knives, agonies, lunchboxes, successes, women, halves, coconuts, magazines*).

Grammar: Possessive Nouns

Aim
- Revise how to use apostrophe ‹s› to show possession and introduce the term *possessive noun*. Refine the children's understanding that nouns sometimes act as adjectives in a sentence.

Introduction
- Briefly revise some of the punctuation the children know (full stops, question marks, exclamation marks, commas, speech marks and apostrophes: see Punctuation, pages 15 to 16) and remind them that punctuation is important because it helps us make sense of the words we use.
- Ask the children when they would use an apostrophe (to show possession or in contractions like *you're*).
- Choose a child, ask him to hold up his pen, and say, *This is [Ben's] pen.* Do this with other children, asking them to hold up things like a book, ruler or pencil and say, *This is [the name of the child]'s.*
- Explain that words with an apostrophe ‹s› that show possession are called possessive nouns.
- Write some examples on the board, showing how to position the apostrophe above the line and in front of the ‹s›. Point out that the apostrophe is needed to show that the ‹s› is not being used to make the plural.

Main Point
- Write the sentence *I ate some of my cake* on the board and parse it with the children. Ask them what kind of word *my* is (a possessive adjective) and underline it in blue. Remind the children that *my* is called a possessive adjective because it is an adjective that describes the cake by saying who it belongs to.
- Replace *my* with *Anna's* and ask the class what is describing the cake now (*Anna's*). Point out that although *Anna's* is a possessive noun, it is acting as an adjective. Explain that possessive nouns always act as adjectives in a sentence.
- Now add *birthday* to the sentence so it reads, *I ate some of Anna's birthday cake.* Remind the children that they already know that nouns can sometimes act as adjectives, as in the compound word *birthday cake* where the first noun *birthday* describes (or modifies) the second noun *cake*.

Activity Page
- The children write inside each outlined apostrophe ‹s›. They then identify the nouns in each sentence, underline them in black, and rewrite the sentences, using the correct possessive nouns (*peacock's tail, model's outfit, genius's ideas, crowd's cheers*).
- Next they write one of the possessive nouns to complete each sentence (*cactus's, pirate's, crocodile's, snowman's*).

Possessive Nouns (Nouns Acting as Adjectives)

REMEMBER Nouns followed by apostrophe ‹s› are called 'possessive nouns'. They are used to show belonging, so rather than saying 'the pen of the boy', we say 'the boy's pen'.

'S 'S 'S 'S 'S 'S 'S 'S 'S 'S 'S 'S 'S 'S 'S 'S 'S

In these sentences, identify the nouns and underline them in black. Then rewrite each sentence using the correct possessive noun. Colour the peacock and its tail when you have finished.

The <u>tail</u> of a <u>peacock</u> is magnificent.

A <u>peacock's tail</u> is magnificent.

Everyone applauded the outfit of the model.

Everyone applauded the _____ _____ .

The ideas of a genius are usually brilliant.

A _____ _____ are usually brilliant.

The cheers of the crowd were very loud.

The _____ _____ were very loud.

Choose a possessive noun to finish each sentence.

The _____ prickles were very sharp.

The _____ ship was huge and menacing.

A _____ teeth are large and strong.

They found traces of the abominable _____ footprints.

snowman's   pirate's   cactus's   crocodile's

Possessive nouns act like adjectives in a sentence. Underline each possessive noun in blue and the noun it is describing in black. Colour the horse and its mane when you have finished.

They came to collect me in Dad's car.

The king's army besieged the castle.

They went to Meg's house for the day.

The horse's mane was very long.

Smoke was coming from the van's engine.

Seth's party was a great success.

21

- Finally, in the last set of sentences, they underline the possessive noun acting as an adjective in blue and the noun it is describing in black (*Dad's car, king's army, Meg's house, horse's mane, van's engine, Seth's party*).

Extension Activity
- Write two lists on the board: one of proper nouns (*Anna, Seth, Meg, Zack, Kate, Sam, Poppy, Mark, Scarlet, Ben, Sue, Jimmy, Jane, Ron, Kitty*) and one of common nouns (*teddy, sandwich, book, nose, vase, cat, jacket, brush, lunch, dog, crayon, hat, teapot, ping pong, apple*).
- The children write as many sentences as they can using the nouns on the board. Each sentence should contain one possessive noun (made from a proper noun) and a common noun. For example, they might use *Zack* and *hat* to make the following sentence: *Zack's hat was blue and pink.*

Rounding Off
- Go over the activity page with the children, checking their answers. If they have done the extension activity, ask some of the children to read out their sentences.

Spelling: Schwa ‹or›

Spelling Test
- The children turn to the backs of their books and find the column labelled *Spelling Test 10*.
- In any order, call out the spelling words learnt last week. The children write the words on the lines.

Revision
- Revise syllables and how to identify them in words by clapping the syllables or doing 'chin bumps' (see Syllables, pages 22 to 23). Remind the children that the number of vowel sounds in a word is the same as the number of syllables.
- Write these words on the board: <u>cel</u>/lar, <u>cus</u>/tard, <u>or</u>/chard, <u>wiz</u>/ard. With the class, identify the vowel sounds, underline the letters making them, separate the words into syllables, and decide which one is stressed.

Spelling Point
- Revise the schwa, which is a swallowed vowel sound that often appears in unstressed syllables. Remind the children that the schwa is the most common vowel sound in English and because it can be the sound of any swallowed vowel, this makes spelling words with a schwa tricky.
- Write the word *ac/tor* on the board and ask the children how many syllables it has (two). Identify the vowel sounds with the class and split the word into two syllables with a line. Say the word with the class, clapping once for each syllable.
- Ask the children which syllable is stressed in <u>actor</u> (the first syllable). Point out that the pure /a/ can be heard in the stressed syllable, whereas the ‹or› in the unstressed syllable sounds more like an /uh/ sound and is therefore a schwa.

Spelling List
- Read the spelling words with the children, go over the meaning of any words they may not know, and ask them to find and highlight the ‹or› saying the schwa in each word. Clap the syllables in each word and see if the children can hear where the stress is.
- Point out the ‹au› spelling in *author*, how the 'magic' in the schwa makes the preceding vowel say its long vowel sound in *motor*, *razor*, *calculator* and *escalator*, but not in *memory*, *visitor* and *decoration*; also point out that the 'magic' from other vowels has the same effect in *senior*, *calculator*, *decoration* and *opportunity*.

author
error
doctor
motor
actor
terror
comfort
senior
razor
mirror
memory
stubborn
calculator
visitor
collector
escalator
decoration
opportunity

Activity Page
- The children choose twelve words from the spelling list and write a sentence for each one.
- They then look at the adjective *stubborn* and write its comparative (*stubborner*) and superlative (*stubbornest*) in the elephants.
- The children then write down the comparative and superlative for each adjective (*bigger, biggest; heavier, heaviest; huger, hugest; broader, broadest*).
- Remind the children they will need to use the spelling rules for adding ‹-er› and ‹-est›.
- Finally, they parse the sentence, underlining each part of speech in the correct colour, identify the subject (*doctor*) and choose the correct tense, which is the past continuous so all parts of the verb should be underlined in red.

The senior doctor was making a correct diagnosis.

Dictation
- Dictate the following sentences:

1. The beautiful woman looked in the mirror.
2. He made an error when he used the calculator.
3. The visitors took the escalator to the next floor.

Grammar: *Present Participles used as Adjectives*

Aim
- Refine the children's knowledge of the present participle and develop their awareness that it can act as an adjective in sentences.

Introduction
- Briefly revise the suffixes that can be added to verbs: ‹-s› or ‹-ies› is added to make the third person singular in the simple present tense, as in *she runs* or *it flies*; ‹-ed› is added to make the simple past tense of regular verbs; and ‹-ing› is added to make the present participle, which is used to form the continuous tenses, as in *I was walking*; *I am walking*; *I will be walking*. The spelling rules for adding ‹-ing› are as follows:
- If the root verb ends in a consonant which is not immediately after a short vowel sound, simply add the suffix, as in *raining*.
- If the root verb ends in ‹e›, remove it before adding the suffix, as in *smiling*. The only exception is when adding ‹-ing› to a root verb ending in ‹ie›: the ‹ie› is replaced by ‹-y› before the suffix is added, to avoid having two ‹i›s next to each other. This is why the present participle of *to lie* is *lying*, but the simple past is *lied*.
- If the root verb ends with a consonant immediately after a short, stressed vowel sound, double the final consonant before adding ‹-ing›, as in *nodding*.
- If the root verb ends in ‹y›, simply add ‹-ing›, so *play* becomes *playing* and *worry* becomes *worrying*. Although 'shy ‹i›' replaces ‹y› in *worried*, it does not return in *worrying* because it would look odd having two ‹i›s next to each other.

Main Point
- So far the children know that the present participle is used in continuous tenses. However, it can also be used in other ways: acting as an adjective (e.g. *the winding road*) or as a gerund which acts as a noun (e.g. *dancing is fun*).
- Write *The galloping horse raced across the field* on the board. Ask the children to find the verb. They should say *raced,* but they may say *galloping.* Explain that although *galloping* looks like a verb (it is a participle, which is a verb form), here it is acting as an adjective to describe (or modify) the horse. Underline the word *raced* in red, *galloping* in blue and *horse* in black.
- To help the children understand this, say the sentence first without *raced* and then without *galloping.* Point out that without the verb *raced* it becomes a phrase, whereas without the adjective *galloping* it is still a sentence.
- Now write the verb *spell* on the board and ask a child to come up and make the present participle

(*spelling*). Ask the children what the word *spelling* could describe and write examples on the board: *spelling test, spelling list, spelling book, spelling lesson, spelling sheet.*

Activity Page
- The children look at each sentence and underline the present participle acting as an adjective in blue and the noun it is describing in black (*screaming boy, chiming clock, drying clothes, amusing tales, irritating fly, bouncing ball*). Remind the children to try saying the sentences without the ‹-ing› word to check that they are still sentences.
- Then they think of nouns that the present participles in the caterpillars could be describing and write them in. They then choose four of these nouns and present participles and put them in sentences.

Extension Activity
- Write some more present participles on the board, such as: *crawling, missing, fighting, annoying, burning, dancing, flashing, floating, flying, grinning, glowing, hurrying, marching, jumping, rocking, snoring, visiting, whispering.* Ask the class to think of a noun that each one could describe.

Rounding Off
- Go over the activity page with the children, asking some to read out their sentences.

Spelling: Schwa ‹er›

Spelling Test
- The children turn to the backs of their books and find the column labelled *Spelling Test 11*.
- Call out the spelling words learnt last week.

Revision
- Revise syllables and how to identify them in words by clapping the syllables or doing 'chin bumps' (see Syllables, pages 22 to 23). Remind the children that the number of vowel sounds in a word is the same as the number of syllables.
- Write these words on the board: *doc/tor, ra/zor, stub/born, mo/tor*. With the class, identify the vowel sounds, underline the letters making them, separate the words into syllables, and decide which one is stressed. Point out that the first syllable in *razor* and *motor* is an open syllable because it ends in the vowel letter saying its long vowel sound.

Spelling Point
- Revise the schwa, which is a swallowed vowel sound that often appears in unstressed syllables. Remind the children that the schwa is the most common vowel sound in English and it can be the sound of any swallowed vowel.
- Write the word *pat/tern* on the board and ask the children how many syllables it has (two). Identify the vowel sounds with the class and split the word into two syllables with a line.
- Say the word with the class, clapping once for each syllable. Ask the children which syllable is stressed in *pattern* (the first).
- Point out that the pure /a/ can be heard in the stressed syllable, whereas the ‹er› in the unstressed syllable sounds more like an /uh/ sound and is therefore a schwa.

Spelling List
- Read the spelling words with the children and ask them to find and highlight the ‹er› saying the schwa in each word. Clap the syllables in each word and see if the children can hear where the stress is.
- Point out the soft ‹g› in *general*, *average* and *exaggerate* and the soft ‹c› in *rhinoceros*.
- Remind the children that in *average* the ‹e› in ‹ge› is also a 'magic ‹e›', making the short vowel in front of the ‹g› into a long one, although because it is unstressed the last syllable sounds more like /ij/.
- Also point out the ‹ea› saying /e/ in *weather*, the silent ‹h› in *whether*

pattern
referee
opera
cavern
modern
manners
general
interest
average
weather
different
interrupt
exaggerate
whether
caterpillar
desperate
rhinoceros
temperature

and *rhinoceros*, ‹a› saying the schwa in *desperate* and ‹ture› in *temperature* saying /cher/.
- Make sure the children understand the difference between the homophones *weather* and *whether*.

Activity Page
- The children unscramble the letters in the caterpillars to make the spelling words (*referee, whether, pattern, caterpillar, modern, manners, weather, general, interrupt, different, average, interest, exaggerate, cavern, desperate, rhinoceros, opera, temperature*).
- They then add the correct punctuation to the three sentences (1. *"It is Anna's turn to sing," announced Miss Beech.* 2. *Grandma exclaimed, "That was beautiful!"* 3. *"Whose turn is it next?" enquired Seth.*).
- The children then write a sentence for each of the punctuation marks shown.
- Finally, they parse the sentence, identify the subject (*archer*) and choose the correct tense (simple future). *Archery* is a noun acting as an adjective. An <u>expert</u> <u>archer</u> <u>will referee</u> the <u>archery</u> <u>competition</u>.

Dictation
- Dictate the following sentences:

1. The author has a particular interest in caverns.
2. The two caterpillars had different patterns.
3. Be careful not to interrupt the lesson.

Grammar: Comparatives and Superlatives (1)

Aim
- Develop the children's knowledge of comparative and superlative adjectives, so they know when to use *more* and *most*, *less* and *least*.

Introduction
- Remind the children that adjectives are words that describe nouns or pronouns. The colour for adjectives is blue. For the action, the children touch the side of one temple with their fist.
- Remind the children that comparative and superlative adjectives describe something by making a comparison. They are formed by adding the suffix ‹-er› to make a comparative and ‹-est› to make a superlative, as in *pink, pinker, pinkest*.
- Discuss how to make the comparative and superlative for the following words, referring to the spelling rules (see pages 24 to 25): *hot* (*hotter, hottest*), *close* (*closer, closest*), *short* (*shorter, shortest*), *happy* (*happier, happiest*), *grey* (*greyer, greyest*).
- Remind the children that if a superlative is used in a sentence, the definite article *the* is needed, as in *This is the biggest elephant.*

Main Point
- Now write *He is an intelligent boy* on the board, and underline the adjective (*intelligent*) in blue. Ask the children how they would make the comparative and superlative for this word. Discuss why 'intelligenter' and 'intelligentest' do not sound right.
- Tell the children that longer adjectives often use the words *more* and *most* to form their comparatives and superlatives, instead of adding a suffix. Explain that short adjectives of one or two syllables tend to take the ‹-er› and ‹-est› suffixes, whereas longer ones often use the words *more* and *most*: so we say *smarter* and *smartest*, but *more intelligent* and *most intelligent*.
- However, sometimes two-syllable adjectives also make their comparative and superlative by adding *more* and *most*, especially ones which have a suffix (e.g. *most helpful, more hopeless, most boring, more worried* and *most famous*). The children need to decide which sounds right.
- Call out the following sentences and ask the children to form the comparatives and superlatives for the adjectives: *It was an **expensive** ring; He was a **beautiful** horse; She was a **helpful** friend.*
- Explain that the antonyms of *more* and *most* are *less* and *least*. With that in mind, ask the children how they would say the opposite of *He is a **more** intelligent boy* and *He is the **most** intelligent boy* (*He is a **less** intelligent boy* and *He is the **least** intelligent boy*).
- This is true for all comparatives and superlatives, however long or short the adjective is. Therefore, as well as *less intelligent* and *least intelligent* we can say *less smart* and *least smart*.

Activity Page
- The children write inside the outlined *Adjectives*, using a blue pencil. They then read the sentences underlining the adjectives in blue (*successful, difficult, interesting, dangerous, important*).
- Then they rewrite each sentence, first with the comparative and then with the superlative, choosing either *more* and *most* or *less* and *least*. Remind the children to use the definite article *the* when using the superlative.
- The children decide whether ‹-er› and ‹-est› or *more* and *most* are used to make the comparatives and superlatives of the adjectives in the chart, putting a tick in the correct box for each one: *safe* (‹-er›/‹-est›), *famous* (more/most), *careful* (more/most), *lazy* (‹-er›/‹-est›), *delicious* (more/most), *short* (‹-er›/‹-est›), *big* (‹-er›/‹-est›), *silly* (‹-er›/‹-est›), *brilliant* (more/most), *thin* (‹-er›/‹-est›).

Extension Activity
- The children use *less* and *least* to make the opposite comparatives and superlatives of those in the table.

Rounding Off
- Go over the children's work, checking their answers.

Spelling: ‹or› saying /er/

Spelling Test
- The children turn to the backs of their books and find the column labelled *Spelling Test 12*.
- In any order, call out the spelling words learnt last week. The children write the words on the lines.

Revision
- Revise the schwa, which is a swallowed vowel sound that often appears in unstressed syllables. The schwa is the most common vowel sound in English and it makes spelling words tricky as it can be the sound of any swallowed vowel.
- Write these words on the board and identify the schwa in each one: **a**void, lem**o**n, fung**u**s, doll**ar**, act**or**, mod**er**n. Blend and sound out the words with the class, saying the schwas in their pure form to help remember the spelling.

Spelling Point
- Revise the main ways of writing the /er/ sound: ‹er›, ‹ir›, ‹ur›. Ask the children to suggest words for each alternative spelling and write them on the board.
- Now write *worm* on the board. Ask the class which letters are making the /er/ sound (‹or›). Sound it out slowly with the children, /w-er-m/. Explain that in some words ‹or› makes the /er/ sound rather than the usual /or/ sound.
- Write *word*, *world* and *work* on the board. Blend and sound them out with the class and identify the ‹or› saying /er/ in each one. Point out that ‹or› follows ‹w› in each word. Remind them that when ‹a› follows ‹w› in *swan*, *wasp* and *swallow*, the ‹a› says the /o/ sound. Similarly, ‹w› can make ‹or› say /er/.

Spelling List
- Read the spelling words with the children, go over the meaning of any words they may not know, and ask them to find and highlight the ‹or› saying /er/ in each word.
- Point out any schwas, such as the ‹er› in *worker*, the ‹se› saying /s/ in *worse*, the suffixes in *work**able***, *worth**less***, *worldli**ness*** and *worthless**ness***, the ‹y› saying /ee/ on the end of *worthy*, the ‹i_e› saying /ie/ in *fireworks*, *worldwide* and *worthwhile*, the soft ‹c› in *workforce* and the ‹wh› in *worthwhile*.
- It is a good idea to blend and sound out the spelling words quickly every day with the children.

worm
word
world
worst
worker
worse
workable
worthy
worship
fireworks
worksheet
worthless
workmanship
worldliness
workforce
worldwide
worthwhile
worthlessness

Activity Page
- The children write the meanings for twelve of the spelling words and use a dictionary to check that they are correct. They then look at the adjectives *worthy*, *worthwhile* and *interesting* and write their comparatives (*worthier*, *more/less worthwhile*, *more/less interesting*) and superlatives (*worthiest*, *most/least worthwhile*, *most/least interesting*) in the elephants. They then make compound words by matching each bird with the correct tail feathers (*world: wide*, *work: out*, *word: search*).
- Finally, they parse the sentence, identify the subject (*He*) and choose the correct tense, which is the simple future so all parts of the verb should be underlined in red.

  He will be the worst worker in the world.

Dictation
- Dictate the following sentences:

1. The workmanship of the artist is spectacular.
2. Worms are found in most parts of the world.
3. "Are these albums worth much?" asked the collector.

Extension Activity
- The children think of as many words as possible that can be added to *worm* to make compound words (examples include: *earthworm*, *wormhole*, *glowworm*, *bookworm*, *inchworm*).

Grammar: Changing Verb Tenses (1)

Aim
• Reinforce the children's knowledge of the simple and continuous tenses and develop their ability to rewrite a sentence in another tense.

Introduction
• Remind the children that verbs can describe what is happening in the past, present or future and can be written in the simple and continuous tenses.
• Revise the actions for verbs (see page 9) and for the tenses (see page 11).

Main Point
• Write *The owl blinks his big round eyes* on the board. Ask which tense the sentence is in (the simple present). Ask the children to identify the verb (*blinks*) and underline it.
• Now ask if anyone can change the tense of the sentence to the simple past. Write *The owl blinked his big round eyes* and remind the children that the simple past of a regular verb is made by adding ‹-ed› to the root word.
• Now ask what the verb would be if the sentence were in the simple future. Write *The owl will blink his big round eyes*, reminding the children that the future is made by adding an auxiliary verb (*shall* or *will*) before the main verb.
• Now ask what the sentence would be in the present continuous. Write *The owl is blinking his big round eyes*, pointing out that the continuous tenses are made with the auxiliary verb *to be* and the present participle (which is made by adding ‹-ing› to the main verb).
• Do this for the past continuous (*was blinking*) and future continuous (*will be blinking*).
• Remind the children that if they rewrite a sentence in the past or continuous tenses, they will need to use the spelling rules for adding ‹-ed› and ‹-ing›, depending on how the root verb is spelt:
- If the root verb ends in a consonant immediately after a short, stressed vowel sound, double the final consonant before adding the suffix, (e.g. *hugged* and *stopping*).
- If the root verb ends in a consonant which is not immediately after a short vowel sound, simply add the suffix (e.g. *rained* and *raining*).
- If the root verb ends in ‹e›, remove it before adding the suffix, (e.g. *smiled* and *smiling*). The only exception is when adding ‹-ing› to a root verb ending in ‹ie›: the ‹ie› is replaced by ‹-y› before the suffix is added, to avoid having two ‹i›s next to each other. That is why the present participle of *to lie* is *lying*, but the simple past is *lied*.
- If the root verb ends in ‹ay›, ‹ey› or ‹oy›, simply add the suffix, (e.g. *played* and *playing*).

- If the root verb ends in a consonant followed by ‹y›, as in *worry*, the spelling rule is different for the two suffixes: 'shy ‹i›' replaces ‹y› in *worried* because ‹i› is no longer at the end of the word, but not in *worrying* as it would look odd having two ‹i›s next to each other.

Activity Page
• The children read the sentences, which are all in the simple present tense, underline the verb in red, and rewrite each sentence using the tense in the bee's banner (simple future: *will exercise*; simple past: *introduced*; past continuous: *were searching*; present continuous: *is rolling*; future continuous: *will be wiping*; simple future: *will cut*; future continuous: *shall/will be starting*; present continuous: *is yawning*; future continuous: *will be camping*; simple present: *are*.
• The children can use the tense tent at the top of the page and the irregular parts of the verb *to be* at the bottom to help them form the verbs correctly.

Extension Activity
• The children rewrite one of the sentences in all six tenses.

Rounding Off
• Go over the children's work, checking their answers.

Spelling: ‹ear› saying /er/

Spelling Test
- The children turn to the backs of their books and find the column labelled *Spelling Test 13*.
- Call out the spelling words learnt last week.

Revision
- Revise the schwa, which is a swallowed vowel sound that often appears in unstressed syllables. The schwa is the most common vowel sound in English and it can be the sound of any swallowed vowel.
- Write these words on the board and identify the schwa in each one: comm**a**, purp**o**se, min**u**s, sug**ar**, doct**or**, ref**er**ee. Blend and sound out the words with the class, saying the schwas in their pure form to help remember the spelling.

Spelling Point
- Remind the children that they know several ways to write the /er/ sound: ‹er›, ‹ir›, ‹ur›, ‹or›. Ask them to suggest some words that contain those spellings and, as each one is called out, ask them which spelling it takes and add it to the appropriate column.
- Remind them that the ‹or› spelling of /er/ always comes after ‹w›, as in *worm*, *word* and *world*.
- Now write *earth* on the board and ask the class which letters are making the /er/ sound (‹ear›).
- Sound the word out slowly with the children, /er-th/, and explain that in some words ‹ear› makes the /er/ sound rather than the usual /ear/ sound.
- Ask the children if they can think of any other words with this spelling and add them to the board. Explain that only a relatively small number of words use the ‹ear› spelling.

Spelling List
- Read the spelling words and ask the children to find and highlight the ‹ear› saying /er/ in each word.
- Point out any schwas, such as the ‹er› in *overheard*, the ‹y› saying /ee/ on the end of *early*, the ‹se› saying /s/ in *hearse* and *rehearse*, the compound words *overheard*, *searchlight*, *earthworm* and *earthquake*, the ‹igh› saying /ie/ in *searchlight*, the ‹or› saying /er/ in *earthworm* and the ‹a_e› saying /ai/ and ‹k› in *earthquake*.

earn
learn
heard
earth
search
earnings
yearn
early
pearl
dearth
hearse
earnest
rehearse
overheard
researcher
searchlight
earthworm
earthquake

Activity Page
- They unscramble the letters and add them to ‹ear› to make words from the spelling list (*earth*, *search*, *heard*, *earnings*, *learn*, *earn*, *hearse*, *early*, *earnest*, *dearth*, *yearn*, *pearl*, *earthworm*, *overheard*, *rehearse*,

earthquake). They then practise writing ‹ear› along the line.
- Then the children use the possessive nouns in the snake to describe the nouns (*the goose's feathers, the author's book, the tree's branches, the referee's decision, the wolf's fur, the expert's opinion*).
- Finally, they parse the sentence, identify the subject (*boys*) and choose the correct tense (past continuous). *Two* is an adjective describing the number of boys. *Intently* is an adverb made by adding ‹-ly› to the adjective *intent* and should be underlined in orange. The two boys were searching intently for earthworms.

Dictation
- Dictate the following sentences:

1. The early bird catches the worm.
2. We learned there was a dearth of pearls.
3. The actors and singers rehearsed the new opera.

Extension Activity
- Write the sentences on the board: *Granny knits a long striped scarf for me; He collects football stickers; They sing in the choir every week; The cat licks its paws.*
- The children underline the verbs in red.
- They could then rewrite the sentences, each in a different tense (simple past, present or future and past, present or future continuous).

Grammar: Homophones (Its and It's)

Aim
- Refine the children's understanding of homophones and develop their ability to choose between similar-sounding words like *its* and *it's* in their writing.

Introduction
- Write *Here is my book and there is yours* on the board. Revise the possessive adjectives (*my, your, his/her/its, our, your, their*), which describe who or what something belongs to. Also revise the possessive pronouns (*mine, yours, his/hers/its; ours, yours, theirs*), which replace a noun and indicate who or what it belongs to.
- Then revise contractions like *you're* and *they're*, which are short for *you are* and *they are*. Remind the children that contractions are mostly used in speech or when writing a friendly note.

Main Point
- Remind the children that it is important to be careful when writing homophones like *our* and *are*, *their*, *there* and *they're*, and *your* and *you're*; although they sound similar to one other, the words have different spellings and meanings. If the wrong homophone is used, the children's writing will not make sense. The children need to stop and think before writing the word, decide which meaning is needed, and think how the word with that meaning is spelt.
- Now write *its* and *it's* on the board and explain that these homophones are also commonly confused in writing. Discuss each one in turn and explain that, like *your* and *you're* and *their* and *they're*, one is a possessive adjective (and in this case also a possessive pronoun, although it is rarely used) and the other is a contraction.
- Ask the children what they think *it's* is short for (it is). Explain that if the homophone in a sentence can be replaced with *it is*, and it makes sense, they should use the contraction. Later they will learn that *it's* can also be short for *it has*.
- Write these two sentences on the board, leaving a space for the homophones: *The dog buried [its] bone behind the bush; [It's] a lovely sunny afternoon.*
- Ask the children which word is needed to complete each sentence.
- Ask the children to suggest some more sentences using *its* and *it's*, write them on the board, and discuss which word is needed in each one.
- Children often find these two homophones particularly difficult, because apostrophe ‹s› can also be used to show possession. However, as the children learnt in their lesson on possessive nouns (see page 21 of the *Grammar 4 Pupil Book*), apostrophe ‹s› is only used to show possession in nouns (e.g.

the **dog's** bone or **Kate's** new hat); because *its* is a possessive adjective (e.g. *the dog chewed **its** bone*), not a possessive noun, it does not need an apostrophe.

Activity Page
- The children write inside the outlined words *its* and *it's* at the top of the sheet and then practise writing the words on the lines.
- They then read the sentences, decide which word(s) are needed to complete each one and write them in (*It's; its, its; it's; its; It's; It's; Its; its; its; It's; It's, its; It's, it's, its*).
- Finally, they write a sentence for each homophone, showing their different meanings.

Extension Activity
- The children write some more sentences of their own with *its* and *it's*. They could work in pairs, taking it in turns to dictate and write down sentences. They then read through the sentences together and decide whether they have used the correct spellings.

Rounding Off
- Go over the activity page with the children, checking their answers. If they have done the extension activity, ask some of the children to read out their sentences.

Spelling: ‹u› saying long /oo/

Spelling Test
- The children turn to the backs of their books and find the column labelled *Spelling Test 14*.
- Call out the spelling words learnt last week.

Revision
- Revise the schwa, which is a swallowed vowel sound that often appears in unstressed syllables. The schwa is the most common vowel sound in English and it makes spelling words tricky as it can be the sound of any swallowed vowel.
- Write these words on the board and identify the schwa in each one: *an**a**gram, sec**o**nd, care**fu**l, bur**gla**r, terr**o**r, cav**e**rn.* Blend and sound out the words with the class, saying the schwas in their pure form to help remember the spelling.

Spelling Point
- Remind the children that although a single vowel letter usually makes a short sound, it can also make a long sound. Sometimes this is because the short vowel sound in one syllable is changed by the 'magic' from the vowel in the next syllable, (e.g. *m**u**sic*). However, sometimes the short vowel letter makes the long vowel sound on its own, without any influence from other vowels, (e.g. *em**u***).
- Now remind the children that the main spellings for the /ue/ sound, which are ‹ue›, ‹ew› and ‹u_e›, can also make the long /oo/ sound (e.g. *true, flew* and *rule*).
- This is also true for ‹u›. Write *truth* on the board, sound it out slowly with the children, /t-r-oo-th/, and underline the ‹u› saying /oo/.

Spelling List
- Read the spelling words with the children, go over the meaning of any words they may not know, and ask them to find and highlight the ‹u› saying /oo/ in each word.
- Point out any schwas, such as the ‹ar› in *lunar*, the silent ‹g› in *gnu*, the ‹y› saying /ee/ on the end of *truly* and *ruby*, the soft ‹c› in *crucial* and *translucent*, the ‹se› saying /s/ in *glucose*, and the soft ‹g› in *plumage*.
- Point out that in *plumage*, the ‹e› in ‹ge› is also a 'magic e'; this makes the short vowel in front of ‹g› (‹a›) into a long vowel. However, because the last syllable is unstressed it sounds more like /ij/.
- It is a good idea to blend and sound out the spelling words quickly every day with the children.

super
ruin
flu
fluid
gnu
truth
truly
cruel
lunar
ruby
fluent
superb
crucial
frugal
glucose
superior
plumage
translucent

Activity Page
- The children read the phrases and decide which words from the spelling list they describe (*super, superb, cruel, plumage, flu, lunar, superior, ruin, ruby, truth, glucose, translucent*). They then write the correct plural for each noun.
- They then write the correct plurals and draw a picture to match each one (*loaves, ponies, crosses, foxes, worms*). Finally, they parse the sentence, identify the subject (*I*) and choose the correct tense, which is the future continuous so all parts of the verb should be underlined in red. *July* is a proper noun and needs a capital letter.

I will be watching the lunar eclipse in July.

Dictation
- Dictate the following sentences:

1. Does the bird have bluish plumage?
2. "I want the truth," said the policeman sternly.
3. They had heard he was fluent in Spanish.

Extension Activity
- Write these plural nouns on the board: *feet, bookshelves, watches, inchworms, toolboxes, rubies, children, pianos, dishes, gnus, pearls, memories.*
- The children write the singular for each plural (*foot, bookshelf, watch, inchworm, toolbox, ruby, child, piano, dish, gnu, pearl, memory*).

Grammar: Plural Subjects and Verbs

Aim
• Develop the children's understanding that when the singular subject of a sentence is made plural, its verb and the rest of the sentence must agree.

Introduction
• Briefly revise plurals and pronouns. Remind the children that personal pronouns can change, depending on whether they are the subject or object of a sentence (subject: *I, you, he/she/it, we, you, they;* object: *me, you, him/her/it, us, you, them*).
• Revise the irregular simple and past tenses of the verb *to be* and conjugate them with the children, doing the pronoun actions (see page 9). The children can find it difficult to recognise the different forms of *to be* in a sentence; regular practice will help.
• Now conjugate a regular verb in the simple present tense (e.g. *to walk*). Remind the children that the suffix ‹-s› is added to the verb after *he, she* and *it,* (e.g. *he walks*).

Main Point
• Write *The lion chases a man* on the board. Ask the children to identify the subject and object of the sentence. To do this, they first need to identify the verb (*chases*). They then have to ask themselves *Who or what chases a man?* to find the subject (*lion*), and *The lion chases what?* to find the object (*man*).
• Remind the children that a sentence always has a verb and subject (the noun or pronoun that 'does' the verb action) but does not necessarily have an object (the noun or pronoun that 'receives' the verb action).
• Ask the children to make the object of the sentence, *man,* plural and change the sentence to *The lion chases a men.* Discuss why this sounds wrong. Remind the children that if they make a singular noun plural, the rest of the sentence must still make sense, or agree.
• The indefinite article *a* is only used with singular nouns, so when a plural noun is used it should be changed to the definite article *the* (which can be used with singular or plural nouns) or something else suitable (e.g. *some, a few* or *three*).
• Now write *The **lions** chases the men.* Ask why this sounds wrong. Explain that the word *lions* is the subject of the sentence, and the verb and subject must always agree. The original sentence is written in the third person singular (the word *lion* can be replaced by *he, she* or *it*) and so the verb takes an ‹-s› ending (e.g. *he chases*). However, because *lions* takes the third person plural form (e.g. *they chase*) the ‹-s› ending is incorrect.
• Write *The lions chase the men* on the board. Check

with the class that everything now makes sense and agrees.

Activity Page
• The children identify the verb in each sentence, underlining it in red.
• They then rewrite the sentences so that the subjects and objects in bold are plural. The children need to make sure that the words that go with the subject and object still make sense and, if not, change them so that they agree. Remind the children that they will have to replace *a* with something that indicates the plural, that the verb must agree with the subject, and that any subject and object pronouns will also need to be made plural (*We, the new watches; hens, lay, the eggs; They, were playing, their guitars; girls, fly, kites; foxes, chase, geese; birds, their nests; We, the large fish*).

Extension Activity
• The children write one or two sentences of their own with a singular subject and object. They then work in pairs, swapping their sentences and rewriting them in the plural.

Rounding Off
• Go over the children's work. If they have done the extension activity, ask some of the children to read out their sentences.

Spelling: ‹ough›, ‹gh› and ‹augh›

Spelling Test
- The children turn to the backs of their books and find the column labelled *Spelling Test 15*.
- Call out the spelling words learnt last week.

Revision
- Revise the schwa, which is a swallowed vowel sound that often appears in unstressed syllables. The schwa is the most common vowel sound in English and it makes spelling words tricky as it can be the sound of any swallowed vowel.
- Write these words on the board and identify the schwa in each one: *husband, handsome, medium, forward, error, whether*. Blend and sound out the words with the class, saying the schwas in their pure form to help remember the spelling.

Spelling Point
- The letters ‹gh› appear in a variety of spelling patterns and sounds in English. So far, the children have learnt that it is in the ‹igh› spelling of /ie/ (e.g. *light, sight, bright*) and is an alternative spelling for the /f/ sound, (e.g. *rough, tough, enough, cough, laugh*). Ask the children to suggest some words for each spelling and write them on the board.
- Now write *bought* and *caught* on the board and sound them out slowly with the class: /b-or-t/ and /c-or-t/. Point out that the ‹gh› is not making either the /ie/ or /f/ sound in these words, but is part of two spellings for the /or/ sound: ‹ough› and ‹augh›.
- Remind the children that *bought* and *caught* are the irregular, or 'tricky', pasts for *buy* and *catch*.
- Explain that ‹ought› and ‹augh› can be used in the spelling of other tricky pasts (e.g. *bring, brought; fight, fought; think, thought; teach, taught*).
- Now write *ghost* on the board and ask what sound the ‹gh› is making here: it is saying /g/, as the ‹h› is silent.
- Explain that ‹g› often appears with a silent ‹h› to say /g/. Point out that other silent letters often go with a particular letter to form a silent letter digraph, such as ‹mb› in *lamb*, ‹kn› in *knee* and ‹wr› in *writer*. The children will look at some of these in later lessons.

Spelling List
- Read the spelling words with the children, and ask them to find and highlight the ‹gh›, ‹ough› or ‹augh› in each word.
- Point out any schwas, such as the ‹a› in *aghast*, the ‹y› saying /ee/ on the end of *ghostly, dinghy*

ought
bought
brought
fought
nought
thought
ghostly
dinghy
ghoul
aghast
gherkin
yoghurt
naughty
fraught
caught
daughter
distraught
onslaught

and *naughty*, the ‹o› saying its long vowel sound in *ghostly*, the ‹ow› saying /oo/ in *ghoul*, the ‹k› spelling in *gherkin* and the ‹ur› spelling of /er/ in *yoghurt*.

Activity Page
- The children fill in the missing letters for each spelling word (*fraught, fought, gherkin, naughty, nought, ghoul, brought, bought, caught, yoghurt, aghast, distraught, onslaught, thought, daughter, ghostly, dinghy, ought*). They then practise writing ‹ought› and ‹augh› on the lines.
- Next they add the correct punctuation to the sentences (1. *"Have you brought the salad?" asked Meg.* 2. *The umpire exclaimed, "Well caught!"* 3. *I bought pickle, ketchup, mustard and some gherkins.*).
- They then use the possessive nouns in the snake to complete the sentences (*loaf's, crocodile's, doctor's, researcher's, pirate's*). Finally, they parse the sentence, identify the subject (*She*) and choose the correct tense (simple past). The adverb *quickly* is made by adding ‹-ly› to the adjective *quick*.
  She quickly caught her naughty daughter.

Dictation
- Dictate the following sentences:

1. The doctor thought that the boy had flu.
2. "That would be my daughter," said Granny.
3. I think they ought to search in the earth.

Grammar: Comparatives and Superlatives (2)

Aim
- Develop the children's understanding that not all comparative and superlative adjectives are made by adding the suffixes ‹-er› and ‹-est›.
- Introduce the comparative and superlative for the adjectives *good* and *bad*.

Introduction
- Remind the children that comparative and superlative adjectives describe something by making a comparison and that they are usually formed by adding the suffix ‹-er› to make a comparative and ‹-est› to make a superlative.
- Write *draughty* on the board and ask the children to call out its comparative (*draughtier*) and superlative (*draughtiest*). Point out that 'shy ‹i›' has replaced 'toughy ‹y›' as it is no longer at the end of the word. Quickly revise the other spelling rules for adding ‹-er› and ‹-est› (see pages 24 to 25).
- Now write *difficult* on the board and ask the children for its comparative (*more difficult*) and superlative (*most difficult*). Remind them that longer words with three or more syllables do not usually use ‹-er› and ‹-est›, but use *more* and *most* in front of the adjective instead. Remind the class that some two syllable adjectives also do this, especially if they have a suffix.
- Write *careless* on the board, identify the suffix (*-less*) and ask how many syllables it has (*two*). Then discuss how to form its comparative and superlative (*more careless; most careless*).

Main Point
- Now write *This is a good story* on the board, identify the adjective (*good*) and underline it in blue. Ask the children how they would make the comparative and superlative for *good*.
- Discuss why neither 'gooder' and 'goodest' and 'more good' and 'most good' sound right. See if any children can think of what they might say instead.
- Explain that the comparative and superlative for *good* are *better* and *best*. Write on the board *This is a better story* and *This is the best story*, and underline the adjectives in blue.
- Now ask the children for the antonym, or opposite, of *good* (*bad*). Write *This is a bad story* on the board. See if the children can suggest the correct comparative (*worse*) and superlative (*worst*) for *bad*.
- Add *This is a worse story* and *This is the worst story* to the board and underline the adjectives in blue.
- Look again at the sentences with *best* and *worst* and point out that the definite article *the* is always used with the superlative.
- Ask the children to think of more nouns that can be

described by *good* or *bad* and ask them for the comparative and superlative for each one.

Activity Page
- The children write inside the outlined word *Adjectives*, using a blue pencil.
- They then read the sentences and identify the adjective *good* or *bad* in each one, underlining it in blue.
- Then they rewrite each sentence, first with the comparative *better* or *worse* and then with the superlative *best* or *worst*.
- Remind the children to use the definite article *the* when using the superlative.

Extension Activity
- The children think of some more sentences that use the adjectives *good* or *bad* to describe a noun.
- They then work in pairs, swapping their sentences and rewriting them using the comparative and superlative.

Rounding Off
- Go over the activity page with the children, checking their answers. If they have done the extension activity, ask some of the children to read out their sentences.

Comparatives and Superlatives — Adjectives

good · better · best · bad · worse · worst

In each sentence, find the adjective and underline it in blue. Then rewrite the sentence twice, first with the appropriate comparative, and then with its superlative.

It was a good day.

He was in a bad mood.

She is a good swimmer.

Dad is a bad dancer.

This is a good book.

That is a bad example.

We are expecting bad weather tomorrow.

They had a good time at the party.

33

Spelling: ‹ive› saying /iv/

Spelling Test
- The children turn to the backs of their books and find the column labelled *Spelling Test 16*.
- Call out the spelling words learnt last week.

Revision
- Revise the schwa, which is a swallowed vowel sound that often appears in unstressed syllables. The schwa is the most common vowel sound in English and it makes spelling words tricky as it can be the sound of any swallowed vowel.
- Write these words on the board and identify the schwa in each one: *magazine, carrot, success, standard, motor, interrupt*. Blend and sound out the words with the class, saying the schwas in their pure form to help them remember the spelling.

Spelling Point
- Revise the ‹se› spelling of the /s/ sound and the ‹ve› spelling of the /v/ sound, which usually come at the end of words. Remind the children that English words rarely end in the letter ‹v›, so if the /v/ sound comes at the end of a word, the spelling is likely to be ‹ve›.
- Write ‹ive› on the board. Ask the children what sound they would normally expect these letters to make at the end of a word. The children will have often seen these letters in words with the 'hop-over ‹e›' digraph ‹i_e›, as in *hive* and *dive*. However, they will also know some words where the same letters say the short vowel sound, as in the verbs *give* and *live*.
- Explain that if the children want to spell a word ending with the sound /iv/, it will probably be spelt ‹ive›.

Spelling List
- Read the spelling words with the children, go over the meaning of any words they may not know, and ask them to find and highlight the ‹ive› in each word.
- Point out the soft ‹g› in *imaginative*. Also point out that the 'magic' from the ‹i› in ‹ive› makes the preceding vowel say its long vowel sound in *motive* and *explosive*, *elusive* and *exclusive* (which are saying the long /oo/ sound rather than /ue/), but not in *positive* or the words ending in ‹ative›. Instead, these vowels have become schwas. It will help the children remember the spellings if they 'say them as they sound', emphasising the pure vowel.

festive
positive
active
massive
negative
motive
adjective
impressive
explosive
elusive
expensive
superlative
constructive
destructive
exclusive
inclusive
alliterative
imaginative

Activity Page
- The children find the spelling words in the word search, looking for words going down as well as across. Next the children write the first letter of their name in the frame. They then write an alliterative sentence, using as many words that begin with that letter as possible.
- They then look at the words in the mirrors and think of a word that means the opposite of each one (possible answers include: *negative: positive, massive: tiny, constructive: destructive, active: inactive, exclusive: inclusive, impressive: unimpressive, imaginative: unimaginative, expensive: inexpensive*). The children may find it helpful to use a thesaurus.
- Finally, they parse the sentence, underlining each part of speech in the correct colour, identify the subject (*They*) and choose the correct tense (present continuous). *Greek* is a proper adjective and needs a capital letter.

They are building an expensive and exclusive hotel on the Greek island.

Dictation
- Dictate the following sentences:

1. That rhinoceros is truly impressive.
2. She wore expensive pearl earrings.
3. "What is an adjective?" asked the teacher.

Grammar: Homophones (To, Too and Two)

Aim
- Refine the children's understanding of homophones and develop their ability to choose between similar-sounding words like *to*, *two* and *too* in their writing.

Introduction
- Revise the possessive adjectives (*my, your, his/her/ its, our, your, their*), which describe who something belongs to. Also revise contractions like *don't* and *can't*, where an apostrophe shows that some letters are missing when a pair of words (like *do not*) are joined together or one longer word (like *cannot*) is shortened.
- Remind the children that they know several possessive adjectives and contractions that make pairs of homophones, such as *its* and *it's*. Children often find these two homophones particularly difficult because apostrophe ‹s› can also be used to show possession. Remind the class that this use of the apostrophe is only used to make possessive nouns (like *the **cat's** fur*) and not possessive adjectives (like, *his, her* and *its*).
- Revise the irregular present tense of the verb *to be* and conjugate it with the children, using the pronoun actions (see Personal Pronouns, page 9).

Main Point
- Remind the children that it is important to be careful when writing homophones like *our* and *are*, *their*, *there* and *they're*, and *your* and *you're*; although they sound similar to one other, the words have different spellings and meanings. If the wrong homophone is used, the children's writing will not make sense. The children need to stop and think before writing the word, decide which meaning is needed, and think about how the word with that meaning is spelt.
- Discuss how the words *our*, *their* and *your* are possessive adjectives that describe who something belongs to, as in *This is our/their/your house*. (*Our* is more properly pronounced /ou-r/ but in practice it is often pronounced /ar/. Emphasise the correct pronunciation for each word when you are talking about *are* and *our* to help the children remember the difference).
- Remind the children that *are* is part of the verb *to be*, and *they're* and *you're* are contractions of *they are* and *you are*. *There* is often used as a pronoun to introduce the subject of a sentence (e.g. *There is our house*) or as an adverb to show position (e.g. *The house is over there*).
- The homophones *to*, *two* and *too* are also commonly confused in writing. Write the words on the board and discuss each one in turn. *To* is used with a verb to make the infinitive (e.g. *to sing*); it is also a

preposition, which is a word that relates one noun or pronoun to another, often by describing where it is or where it is moving towards (e.g. *I am going to the park*). *Two* is the spelling for the number. *Too* is a synonym of *also*.
- Ask the children to suggest sentences using *to*, *two* and *too* and write them on the board, asking which spelling should be used for each one.

Activity Page
- The children write inside the outlined homophones.
- They then read the sentences, decide which homophone(s) are needed to complete each one and cross out the incorrect words (*our; they're; are; their; There, two; you're; are; you're; your; your; their; too; to, our; There; our*).

Extension Activity
- The children think of more sentences of their own for some of the homophones. They could work in pairs, taking it in turns to dictate a sentence, and then decide together whether the correct spelling has been used.

Rounding Off
- Go over the activity page with the children, checking their answers. If they have done the extension activity, ask some of the children to read out their sentences.

Spelling: ‹-ic›

Spelling Test
- The children turn to the backs of their books and find the column labelled *Spelling Test 17*.
- Call out the spelling words learnt last week.

Revision
- Revise the schwa, which is a swallowed vowel sound that often appears in unstressed syllables. The schwa is the most common vowel sound in English and it makes spelling words tricky as it can be the sound of any swallowed vowel.
- Write these words on the board and identify the schwa in each one: *paragraph, method, album, cellar, author, weather*. Blend and sound out the words with the class, saying the schwas in their pure form to help remember the spelling.

Spelling Point
- Revise suffixes, which are usually one or more syllables added at the end of a word to change its meaning. Suffixes can make comparative and superlative adjectives (*bigger, biggest*), plural nouns (*hats, foxes, babies*), the simple past tense (*walked*) and the present participle (*walking*).
- Suffixes can also turn one type of word into another: ‹-y› turns nouns into adjectives and ‹-ly› turns adjectives into adverbs; ‹-ful› and ‹-less› turn abstract nouns into adjectives meaning *without (it)* and *full of (it)*; ‹-able› turns verbs into adjectives meaning being *capable or worthy of being (it)*.
- Write *athletic* on the board. Explain that ‹-ic› is a suffix meaning *related to (it)* and that it is often found in adjectives. It does not take the ‹ck› spelling because it usually only appears in multisyllabic words (multisyllabic words that do end in ‹ck› are usually compound words like *backpack*).
- Not all ‹-ic› words are adjectives: *attic, picnic, medic, music, topic* and *mosaic* are all nouns.

Spelling List
- Read the spelling words with the children and ask them to highlight the ‹ic› spelling in each word.
- Point out any schwas, such as the ‹a› in *dramatic, lunatic, sympathetic* and *characteristic*, how the 'magic' from one vowel makes another vowel say its long vowel sound in *poetic, heroic, chaotic* and *scientific*, the ‹ss› in *classic*, the way ‹ex› in *exotic* sounds more like /egz/, the ‹u› saying /oo/ in *lunatic*, the ‹ch› saying /k/ in *chaotic*

epic
comic
hectic
toxic
classic
exotic
heroic
poetic
athletic
dramatic
fantastic
lunatic
chaotic
rhythmic
scientific
sympathetic
monosyllabic
characteristic

and *characteristic*, the silent letters in *rhythmic* and *scientific*, and the ‹y› saying /i/ in *rhythmic, sympathetic* and *monosyllabic*.

Activity Page
- The children write in the spelling word that completes each sentence (*athletic, toxic, fantastic, classic, scientific, dramatic, rhythmic, sympathetic, hectic, exotic, heroic, monosyllabic*).
- They then read the sentences and cross out the incorrect homophone (*Everybody **knows** the words to the song; **Your** brothers **are** both very athletic; We had to **wait** an **hour** for **our** dinner; The **blue flower** has a lovely **scent**; The students had **to** recite **two** epic poems; **Their** heroic deeds were reported in all the newspapers*).
- Finally, they parse the sentence, identify the subject (*poem*) and choose the correct tense (simple present).

An epic poem is a dramatic story about heroic deeds.

Dictation
- Provide a sheet of paper for each child and dictate the following sentences:

1. There has been a gigantic earthquake.
2. "The fireworks were fantastic!" exclaimed Sam.
3. Recent world events have been very dramatic.

Grammar: Homophones (Where, Wear and Were)

Aim
- Refine the children's understanding of homophones and develop their ability to choose between similar-sounding words like *where*, *wear* and *were* in their writing.

Introduction
- Revise the homophones the children know. Include *to* (a preposition), *two* (a number) and *too* (meaning *also*) and the possessive adjective *its* and contraction *it's* (which is short for *it is*).
- Children often find *its* and *it's* particularly difficult because apostrophe ‹s› can also be used to show possession. Remind the class that this use of the apostrophe is only used to make possessive nouns and not possessive adjectives.
- Revise the irregular past tense of the verb *to be* (*I was, you were, he/she/it was, we were, you were, they were*) and conjugate it with the children, using the pronoun actions (see Personal Pronouns, page 9).

Main Point
- Remind the children that it is important to be careful when writing homophones because although they sound similar to one other, the words have different spellings and meanings; if the wrong one is used, the children's writing will not make sense. The children need to stop and think before writing the word, decide which meaning is needed, and think how the word with that meaning is spelt.
- For example, the words *where*, *wear* and *were* are commonly confused in writing. Write the words on the board and discuss each one in turn.
- *Where* and *wear* are homophones: *where* is one of the ‹wh› question words (*what, why, when, where, who, which, whose*) and refers to place or position. *Wear* is a verb referring to putting on things like clothes and shoes.
- The word *were* is part of the irregular past tense of the verb *to be*; although it is not strictly a homophone of *where*, their spellings are often confused and so it helps to look at them together.
- Write these three sentences on the board, leaving a space for *where*, *wear* and *were*. Ask the children which word to use in each one: *(Where) shall I put this down? We will (wear) our new dresses to the party; They (were) going shopping later.*
- Remind the class to think about what kind of word is missing to help them choose correctly.
- Then ask the children to suggest some more sentences using *where*, *wear* and *were*, write them on the board, and discuss which word to use each time.

Activity Page
- The children write inside the outlined words *where*, *wear* and *were* at the top of the sheet and then practise writing the words on the lines.
- Then they read the sentences, decide which is the correct word (*wear, Where, were, were, wear, Where, were, were, wear, where*), and cross out the wrong ones.
- Finally, they write a sentence for each homophone.

Extension Activity
- The children work in pairs to revise the homophones they have learnt so far.
- Write the following homophones on the board: *our* and *are*; *their, there* and *they're*; *your* and *you're*; *its* and *it's*; *to, two* and *too*; and *where, wear* and *were*.
- The children think of sentences for one set of homophones (e.g. *their, there* and *they're*) to dictate to their partner and together they check whether the correct spellings have been used. They work through as many sets of homophones as they can.

Rounding Off
- Go over the activity page with the children, checking their answers. If they have done the extension activity, ask some of the children to read out their sentences.

Spelling: ‹st› saying /s/

Spelling Test
- The children turn to the backs of their books and find the column labelled *Spelling Test 18*.
- Call out the spelling words learnt last week.

Revision
- Write these words on the board, and blend and sound them out with the class: *worm*, *learn*, *flu*, *ough*t, *festive*, *epic*.
- Identify the various spelling patterns: ‹or› saying /er/, ‹ear› saying /er/, ‹u› saying long /oo/, ‹ough› saying /or/, ‹ive› saying /iv/, and the suffix ‹-ic›.

Spelling Point
- Revise the ‹gh› spelling of /g/ in words like *ghost*, *ghastly* and *yoghurt*. Point out that these words would sound the same with or without ‹h› and so this letter can be thought of as silent.
- Explain that some silent letters often go with a particular letter to form a 'silent letter digraph'. Write these words on the board and ask the children to find the silent letter in each one, as well as the letter it usually accompanies: thu**mb**, **wr**ap, **kn**ot, **wh**ip, **rh**ino, **wh**o, **sc**ent, **gn**aw. Point out that in *whip* the ‹h› is silent and in *who* the ‹w› is silent.
- Now write *castle*, *listen* and *chestnut* on the board and ask the class which silent letter digraph they all have in common: ‹st› saying /s/.

Spelling List
- Read the spelling words with the children, go over the meaning of any words they may not know, and ask them to find and highlight the ‹st› saying /s/ in each word.
- Point out that the last syllable in many of the words is either ‹en› or ‹le›; these are unstressed syllables because of the schwa sound in both.
- Also point out the ‹a› saying /ar/ in *castle* and *fasten* (although in some regions this is pronounced /a/, which makes the spelling straightforward), the ‹a› saying /ai/ in *hasten* and *chasten*, the silent letter digraphs ‹wh› in *whistle* and ‹wr› in *wrestle*, the capital letter at the beginning of the proper noun *Christmas* and the ‹oe› spelling of /oa/ in *mistletoe*.

castle
bustle
listen
thistle
jostle
glisten
bristle
fasten
hasten
moisten
whistle
gristle
Christmas
mistletoe
chestnut
nestle
wrestle
chasten

Activity Page
- The children put the spelling words into alphabetical order (*bristle, bustle, castle, chasten, chestnut, Christmas, fasten, glisten, gristle, hasten, jostle, listen, mistletoe, moisten, nestle, thistle, whistle, wrestle*).

- They then identify the silent letter digraph in each word (**kn**uckle, li**mb**, **wh**ole, de**sc**end, **rh**yme, **kn**eel, desi**gn**, a**sc**end, **wr**ap, **wr**ong, **wr**iggle, **wh**isk, cru**mb**, **gn**aw, **rh**ino). The children then fill in the missing silent letter digraph for each word (**kn**elt, **wr**ist, nu**mb**, **sc**ene, si**gn**, **wr**eck, ca**st**le, **gn**at, thu**mb**, **kn**ight, **sc**ent, to**mb**, gli**st**en, **gn**ome, **wr**ong).
- Finally, they parse the sentence, identify the subject *(I)* and choose the correct tense, which is the simple future so all parts of the verb should be underlined in red. *Christmas* is a proper noun and needs a capital letter.

I will roast chestnuts on the fire at Christmas.

Dictation
- Dictate the following sentences:

1. She ground the spices in the mortar and pestle.
2. "I was jostled in the hustle and bustle," said Bob.
3. They listened for the referee to blow his whistle.

Extension Activity
- The children draw a table with the following column headings: *mb, wr, gn, sc, st, kn, rh, wh*.
- They then sort the words from the last two activities according to their silent letter digraphs, writing them in the correct columns. If they can think of any other words for these silent letter digraphs, they can add them to the correct column.

Grammar: ‹-al› Making Nouns into Adjectives

Aim
- Refine the children's knowledge of suffixes and how they change the meaning of words. Introduce the suffix ‹-al›.

Introduction
- Remind the class that a suffix is usually one or more syllables added at the end of a word to change its meaning. They can make plurals (*hens, benches, ladies*), comparatives and superlatives (*brighter, brightest*), the simple past tense (*I wished*) and the present participle (*wishing*).
- Suffixes sometimes turn one type of word into another: ‹-y› turns nouns into adjectives (*cloudy*) and ‹-ly› turns adjectives into adverbs (*loudly*); ‹-ful› and ‹-less› turn abstract nouns into adjectives (*harmful, harmless*); and ‹-able› turns verbs into adjectives (*breakable*).
- Ask the children which new suffix they have learnt recently. Write *poetic* on the board, underlining ‹ic›. Remind them that ‹-ic› is a suffix often found in adjectives, meaning *related to (it)* or *having the qualities of (it)*; *poetic*, therefore, describes something that has the quality of poetry, as in *poetic language*. Ask the children if they can think of other adjectives ending in ‹-ic› and how they could use them in a sentence.

Main Point
- Introduce the suffix ‹-al›, which can be added to nouns to make adjectives. Write the word *musical* on the board and discuss what it means in phrases like *musical instrument* and *musical laughter*: a piano is an instrument that plays music, and laughter sometimes sound like music, so the suffix ‹-al› makes adjectives meaning *related to (it)* or *having the qualities of (it)*. It refers to the rest of the word, in this case *music*; this is called the root word.
- Explain that if the children read an unfamiliar word, they may be able to guess the meaning if they can recognise the suffix and the meaning of the root word. Write *natural* on the board and ask what the root word is (*nature*). See whether the children know what *natural* means when it is used in a sentence. Point out that ‹-al› starts with a vowel, so the ‹e› at the end of *nature* is removed before adding the suffix. (If ‹e› is part of soft ‹c›, as in *finance*, it is removed and ‹-ial› is added, as in *financial*.)
- The same is true for root words ending in ‹a›, such as *flora*, which becomes *floral*. *Flora* means *flowers*, so *floral* describes things that are decorated with real flowers or pictures of flowers, as in *a floral display* or *an old floral carpet*.
- If the root word ends in a consonant immediately before ‹y›, as in *territory*, 'toughy ‹y›' is replaced

with 'shy ‹i›' before adding ‹-al›, as in *territorial*.
- Point out that both ‹-ic› and ‹-al› make adjectives with a similar meaning.
- Write *typical* on the board and ask what the root word is (*type*). Point out that some adjectives have both suffixes, ‹-ic› and ‹-al›. (These are not to be confused with words like *musical*, where ‹ic› is part of the root word.) Sometimes such adjectives can end in either ‹-ic› or ‹-ical›, as in *rhythmic* and *rhythmical*. Here the meaning is the same but sometimes it can be slightly different, as in *historic* and *historical*.

Activity Page
- The children write the root word for each adjective (*flora, accident, logic, intention, critic, coast*).
- Next they make the nouns in the fish into adjectives, add them to the correct sentences (*tropical, orchestral, bridal, musical, fictional, additional, traditional, natural, magical, hexagonal*).
- Finally, the children write the root word for the three adjectives ending in ‹-ical› (*alphabet, rhythm, myth*).

Extension Activity
- Write some nouns on the board and ask the children to make them into adjectives by adding ‹-al› or ‹-ical›: *medic(al), clinic(al), tactic(al), bacteria (bacterial), condition(al), globe (global), form(al), history (historical), sphere (spherical)*.

Suffix ‹-al› Making **Nouns** into **Adjectives**

Some adjectives are made by adding ‹-al› to a noun.
Look at the examples below and write down the noun that is the root word for each adjective.

Adjectives	floral	accidental	logical	intentional	critical	coastal
Nouns						

Make the noun in each fish body into an adjective and complete the sentences.

addition bride tropic -al
nature fiction tradition
magic hexagon music orchestra

The papaya is a _____ fruit.

The flute is an _____ instrument.

A _____ gown is another name for a wedding dress.

There are several singers in Mary's _____ family.

Sherlock Holmes is a famous _____ detective.

I asked for an _____ ticket to the concert.

The dancers wore _____ Spanish costumes.

Wool, cotton, silk and linen are all _____ materials.

He told a tale of dragons, unicorns and other _____ creatures.

Honeycombs have _____ cells where bees store their honey.

Sometimes the suffix ‹-ic› is put in front of ‹-al› when it is added to a noun to make an adjective.
Write down the noun that is the root word for each of the adjectives below.

alphabetical _____   rhythmical _____   mythical _____

_____   _____   _____

39

Spelling: Silent Letters

Spelling Test
- The children turn to the backs of their books and find the column labelled *Spelling Test 19*.
- In any order, call out the spelling words learnt last week. The children write the words on the lines.

Revision
- Write these words on the board, and blend and sound them out with the class: *word, **ear**th, **s**uper, **fough**t, act**ive**, exot**ic**.*
- Identify the various spelling patterns: ‹or› saying /er/, ‹ear› saying /er/, ‹u› saying long /oo/, ‹ough› saying /or/, ‹ive› saying /iv/, and the suffix ‹-ic›.

Spelling Point
- Remind the children that some silent letters often go with a particular letter to form a silent letter digraph.
- Write these words on the board and ask the children to find the silent letter in each one, as well as the letter it usually accompanies: *la**mb**, **wr**ist, **kn**ew, **wh**at, **rh**ythm, **wh**ose, **sc**ene, **gn**u, **gh**oul, gli**st**en.*
- Point out that in *what* the ‹h› is silent and in *whose* the ‹w› is silent.

Spelling List
- Read the spelling words with the children, go over the meaning of any words they may not know, and ask them to find and highlight the silent letter digraph in each word.
- Point out any schwas, such as the ‹a› in *ascend*, the ‹ir› spelling of /er/ in *whirl*, the ‹ck› in *wreck* and *buckle*, the antonyms *ascend* and *descend*, the ‹n› saying /ng/ in *wrangle* as the ‹g› is spoken, the ‹se› saying /s/ and ‹ere› saying /air/ in *elsewhere*, the way the ‹cc› in *succumb* stops the 'magic' from the second ‹u› changing the short vowel sound of the first ‹u›, and the superlative adjective *wrinkliest*.
- It is a good idea to blend and sound out the spelling words quickly every day with the children.

whirl
wreck
kneel
crumb
ascend
descend
wrangle
knuckle
limb
gnarled
plumbing
elsewhere
ghoulish
succumb
fascinate
wrinkliest
overwhelm
dumbfounded

Activity Page
- The children read the phrases and decide which words from the spelling list they describe (*limb, ascend, wrinkliest, crumb, succumb, elsewhere, fascinate, whirl, gnarled, descend, dumbfounded, knuckle*).
- They then write the meanings for the pairs of homophones, *muscle* and *mussel*, and *knight* and *night*.

- Finally, they parse the sentence, underlining each part of speech in the correct colour, identify the subject (*limbs*) and choose the correct tense, which is the past continuous so all parts of the verb should be underlined in red.

The knotty limbs of the gnarled tree were growing in fantastic shapes.

Dictation
- Provide a sheet of paper for each child and dictate the following sentences:

1. They were dumbfounded by the magic show.
2. The thistle does not have any scent.
3. "I ought to fix the plumbing," said Roy.

Extension Activity
- Write these words on the board: *du**mb**, nu**mb**, **wr**eath, **kn**ack, **wr**ing, to**mb**, **wh**iff, cre**sc**ent.*
- The children look up the words in a dictionary and write down their meanings. They then identify the silent letter digraph in each one.

Grammar: Plural Possessive Nouns

Aim
- Develop the children's ability to form plural possessive nouns and to understand the difference between a plural possessive and a plural noun.

Introduction
- Briefly revise apostrophes and how they can be used in contractions like *you're* or in possessive nouns like *Dad's*.
- Choose a child, ask her to hold up her book, and say, *This is [Anna's] book.* Do this with other children, asking them to hold up things like their pens, rulers or pencils and say, *This is [the name of the child]'s*. Write some examples on the board (e.g. *Kate's, Tim's, Polly's*), showing how to position the apostrophe above the line and in front of the ‹s›.
- Now write some regular plurals on the board and discuss how each one is made: *hills, glasses, tomatoes, studios, keys, teddies*. Finally write some irregular plurals on the board and discuss what makes them tricky: *wives, deer, teeth, children*.

Main Point
- Remind the children that punctuation is important because it helps us make sense of the words we use.
- Write *trees* and *tree's* on the board and ask the children to describe the difference between them: the suffix ‹-s› in *trees* shows that it is the plural of *tree*, meaning that there is more than one tree; the apostrophe ‹-s› in *tree's* shows that it is a possessive noun and is used to describe something belonging to the tree, such as its leaves, trunk or branches.
- Ask the children to use each word in a sentence (e.g. *The trees in the forest are very old* and *The tree's leaves turned red, yellow and orange*). Discuss the difference in meaning.
- Now ask the children what would happen if they wanted to talk about the leaves of more than one tree; how would they write the plural possessive noun? If they were to add apostrophe ‹-s› to *trees*, it would become *trees's*.
- Try saying *Many trees's leaves turned red.* Discuss why this does not sound right. Explain that because the plural already ends in ‹s›, the possessive noun is made by adding only the apostrophe.
- Write *Many trees' leaves turned red* on the board and show the children how to position the apostrophe after the ‹s›.
- Now discuss how they might form the possessive plural of an irregular noun like *children*. Say *the children's toys* and ask them to listen carefully for the ‹s› in *children's*.
- Explain that if irregular plurals do not end in ‹s›, their possessive nouns are formed like singular

possessives: by adding apostrophe ‹s›.
- However, irregular plurals that do end in ‹s›, like *wolves*, make possessive nouns like other plural possessives, by just adding the apostrophe.

Activity Page
- The children look at each word and write its plural noun and then its possessive noun (*cars, cars'; ponies, ponies'; buses, buses'; heroes, heroes'; calves, calves'; men, men's*).
- Next they read the sentences, decide whether the missing words are plural nouns or plural possessives and write them in (*babies', babies, cats, cats', actresses', actresses, geese's, geese, Smiths', Smiths; boys', boys*).

Extension Activity
- Write some more nouns on the board and ask the children to write the plurals. Then ask them to make the plurals into possessive nouns and use them in a sentence.

Rounding Off
- Go over the activity page with the children, checking their answers. If they have done the extension activity, ask some of the children to read out their sentences.

Spelling: ‹-ically›

Spelling Test
- The children turn to the backs of their books and find the column labelled *Spelling Test 20*.
- Call out the spelling words learnt last week.

Revision
- Write these words on the board, and blend and sound them out with the class: *world, heard, truth, caught, massive, poetic.*
- Identify the various spelling patterns: ‹or› saying /er/, ‹ear› saying /er/, ‹u› saying long /oo/, ‹augh› saying /or/, ‹ive› saying /iv/, and the suffix ‹-ic›.

Spelling Point
- Remind the children that when a suffix is used in a word, the rest of the word is called the root and that the suffixes ‹-ic› and ‹-al› can both be used to make adjectives meaning *related to* or *having the qualities of* the root word.
- Write the words *theatrical* and *rhythmical* on the board and point out that some adjectives have both suffixes. (These are not to be confused with a word like *musical* where ‹ic› is part of the root word.)
- Sometimes such adjectives can end in either ‹-ic› or ‹-ical›, as in *rhythmic* and *rhythmical*. Here the meaning is the same but sometimes it can be slightly different, as in *historic* and *historical*.
- Explain that adverbs ending in ‹-ically› can be made from these types of adjectives: if the adjective ends in ‹-ical›, ‹-ly› is added in the usual way, but if it ends in ‹-ic›, ‹-ally› is added instead.

Spelling List
- Read the spelling words with the children, and ask them to find and highlight ‹-ically› in each word.
- Point out the soft ‹g› in *logically*, the ‹ch› spelling of /k/ in *technically* and *chaotically*, the ‹y› saying /i/ in *typically* and *rhythmically*, the ‹ph› saying /f/ in *alphabetically* and *catastrophically*, the ‹au› spelling in *traumatically* and the silent letter digraph ‹rh› in *rhythmically*.
- Also point out how ‹zz› in *quizzically* stops the 'magic' from the second ‹i› changing the short vowel sound of the first ‹i›, but because there is no consonant doubling in *basically, romantically* and *chaotically*, the short vowel becomes long.

artistically
critically
logically
quizzically
basically
vertically
historically
politically
romantically
technically
typically
chaotically
alphabetically
traumatically
majestically
rhythmically
sarcastically
catastrophically

Activity Page
- The children write the adjective and the adverb for each of the nouns. The adjectives use the suffixes ‹-al›, ‹-ic› or ‹-ical› (*logical, artistic, quizzical, critical, technical, chaotic, typical, romantic, majestic, sarcastic, traumatic, rhythmic(al), basic, natural, alphabetic(al), accidental*) and the adverbs are then made by adding either ‹-ly› or ‹-ally›.
- They then complete each sentence by writing the missing homophone (*were, where, wear*). Finally, they parse the sentence, identify the subject (*queen*) and choose the correct tense (simple past). *Highest* is the superlative of the adjective *high* and *castle* is a noun acting as an adjective.

The <u>queen</u> <u>waved</u> <u>majestically</u> <u>from</u> the <u>highest</u> <u>castle</u> <u>window</u>.

Dictation
- Dictate the following sentences:

1. She spoke poetically about her homeland.
2. The wizard vanished magically in a puff of smoke.
3. "The meeting ended chaotically," said the reporter.

Extension Activity
- The children write the adjective and adverb for each of these root words: *history* (*historic, historically*), *fate* (*fatal, fatally*), *continue* (*continual, continually*), *catastrophe* (*catastrophic, catastrophically*).

Grammar: Root Words, Prefixes and Suffixes

Aim
- Refine the children's ability to identify the root word, prefix and suffix in a word. Develop their understanding that words can have more than one prefix and suffix.

Introduction
- Remind the class that prefixes and suffixes are usually one or more syllables added at the beginning (prefixes) and end (suffixes) of a word to change or add meaning.
- Suffixes can make plurals (*hens*, *benches*, *ladies*), comparatives and superlatives (*brighter*, *brightest*), the simple past tense (*wished*) and the present participle (*wishing*).
- They sometimes turn one type of word into another: ‹-y›, ‹-al›, ‹-ic› and ‹-ical› can turn nouns into adjectives (*cloudy*, *traditional*, *poetic*, *typical*); ‹-ly› turns adjectives into adverbs (*loudly*); ‹-ful› and ‹-less› turn abstract nouns into adjectives (*harmful*, *harmless*); and ‹-able› turns verbs into adjectives (*breakable*).
- Write these words on the board: *impatient*, *undo*, *nonstop* (which all mean *not*), *decode*, *disappear* (which both mean *undo*), *misunderstood* (*wrongly* or *not*), *refill* (*again*), *midway* (*middle*), *semicircle* (*half*). Revise the prefixes and discuss the meanings.

Main Point
- Write these words on the board and ask the children if they have a suffix or a prefix: *sadness*, *painter*, *uncertain*, *midday*, *kindly*, *accidental*, *redo*, *devalue*.
- Ask the children if they can remember what the rest of a word is called (root word). Remind them that knowing the meaning of a suffix or prefix and the root word can usually help them understand the meaning of an unfamiliar word.
- Now write *avoid* on the board and ask the children what it means (to keep away from or to stop something from happening). Add the suffix ‹-able›. Discuss how the word now means *able to be avoided*. Then add the prefix ‹-un› to give it the opposite meaning. Finally, add the suffix ‹-ly› to make the adverb *unavoidably* and ask the children to use it in a sentence (e.g. *We were unavoidably late for our meeting*).
- Ask how many prefixes and suffixes *unavoidably* has and explain that words can have more than one of each. Also point out that the ‹-le› in *unavoidable* is removed before the suffix ‹-ly› is added.
- Remind the children of other spelling rules for adding suffixes, while writing these words on the board: *silliness*, *funny*, *finished*, *nicer*, *traceable*, *financial*, *lying*. Identify the suffixes with the class and go over the spelling rules for each one.

Root Words, Prefixes and Suffixes

Activity Page
- The children join the root words to their prefixes or suffixes to make new words (*happiness*, *hopeful*, *singer*, *comfortable*, *cheerful*, *sunny*, *unkind*, *recycle*).
- They then divide words into their root words and prefixes or suffixes. Prefixes should be written in the fish's head, suffixes in the tail and root words in the body (*mid/night*, *paint/ing*, *quick/ly*, *mis/behave*, *semi/final*, *im/mature*, *non/sense*, *beauty/ful*).
- Finally, they make new words by joining each root word to both a prefix and a suffix (*unmissable*, *rediscovery*, *unremarkable*, *comfortably*, *hurriedly*, *unrhythmically*).
- Sometimes there will be more than one prefix or suffix. Remind the children that they will need to use the spelling rules when they add a suffix.

Extension Activity
- Write these words on the board: *thankful*, *banker*, *darkness*, *fashionable*, *airy*, *untidy*, *return*, *nonstop*, *semicircle*, *misplace*, *unsuitable*, *critically*, *unexpectedly*, *disrespectful*, *rebuilding*.
- The children identify the root word and any prefixes and/or suffixes by drawing a circle around each part of the word (*thank/ful*, *bank/er*, *dark/ness*, *fashion/able*, *air/y*, *un/tidy*, *re/turn*, *non/stop*, *semi/circle*, *mis/place*, *un/suit/able*, *critic/al/ly*, *un/expect/ed/ly*, *dis/respect/ful*, *re/build/ing*).

Spelling: Schwa ‹al›

Spelling Test
- The children turn to the backs of their books and find the column labelled *Spelling Test 21*.
- Call out the spelling words learnt last week.

Revision
- Revise the schwa, which is a swallowed vowel sound that often appears in unstressed syllables. The schwa is the most common vowel sound in English and it makes spelling words tricky as it can be the sound of any swallowed vowel.
- Write these words on the board and identify the schwa in each one: *panda, button, cactus, sugar, actor, pattern*. Blend and sound out the words with the class, saying the schwas in their pure form to help remember the spelling.

Spelling Point
- Revise the ‹le› spelling, which comes at the end of multisyllabic words. It sounds something like /ool/ as it has a small schwa before the /l/.
- Write *candle*, *simple* and *puzzle* on the board; say them with the class, clapping once for each syllable. See if the children can hear the schwa in the second unstressed syllable.
- Now write *total*, *camel* and *pencil* on the board. Point out that the ‹al›, ‹el› and ‹il› at the end of these words has the same /ool/ sound as ‹le›, because the vowel in these unstressed syllables is a schwa. Explain that there is no rule for which vowels should be used and so the spellings have to be learnt.
- Remind the children that the suffix ‹al› can be added to nouns to make adjectives like *bridal*, but it is important to remember that not all words ending in ‹al› are adjectives.

Spelling List
- Read the spelling words with the children, go over the meaning of any words they may not know, and ask them to find and highlight the ‹al› spelling in each word.
- Remind them that, like other vowels, the 'magic' of the schwa in ‹al› can change a short stressed vowel in the previous syllable into the long vowel sound, as in *plural, total, equal, casual* and *natural*.
- Notice how the ‹e› in *cathedral* makes the /ee/ sound on its own, and is not influenced by the schwa, because ‹dr› is blocking the 'magic'.
- Point out the soft ‹c› in *special*, the schwa in *several*, the ‹y›

animal
coral
special
plural
total
equal
external
several
crystal
casual
capital
hospital
abysmal
natural
journal
festival
material
cathedral

saying /i/ in *crystal* and *abysmal*, the ‹s› saying /zh/ in *casual*, the ‹s› saying /z/ in *abysmal*, the ‹our› saying /er/ in *journal* and the ‹er› saying /ear/ in *material*. It is a good idea to blend and sound out the spelling words quickly every day, emphasising the /a/ in ‹al› to help remember the spelling.

Activity Page
- The children choose twelve words from the spelling list and write a sentence for each one. They then write the correct plural possessive to complete each sentence (*Chameleons', ladies', children's*).
- They then complete the sentences with singular or plural possessives (*bees', bird's, dogs'*).
- Finally, they parse the sentence, identify the subject (*They*) and choose the correct tense, which is the future continuous so all parts of the verb should be underlined in red.

They will be taking photos of the colossal and monumental cathedral.

Dictation
- Provide a sheet of paper for each child and dictate the following sentences:

1. She accidentally broke the crystal vase.
2. They listened for the animals in total silence.
3. "The festival was terrifically busy!" exclaimed Ray.

Grammar: Grammatical Person

Aim
- Refine the children's knowledge of personal pronouns. Introduce the terms *first*, *second* and *third person* and explain that they can be singular or plural.

Introduction
- Briefly revise pronouns. Pronouns are short words that replace nouns and the colour for them is pink. So far the children have learnt the personal pronouns (*I, you, he/she/it, we, you, they*) and the possessive pronouns (*mine, yours, his/hers/its, ours, yours, theirs*).
- Remind the class that personal pronouns can change depending on whether the noun they are replacing is the subject (*I, you, he/she/it, we, you, they*) or object (*me, you, him/her/it, us, you, them*) of a sentence. Practise saying the different kinds of pronoun with the class using the pronoun actions (see Personal Pronouns, page 9).

Main Point
- Tell the children that personal pronouns are called 'personal' because they mostly relate to people.
- If you talk about yourself, or about yourself and others, you use *I* and *we*. If you talk directly to one or more people, you call them *you*, and if you talk about someone or something else, you use *he, she* and *it* for the singular and *they* for the plural.
- Explain that these three groups are known as first, second and third person and they can be singular or plural: *I* is the first person singular and *we* is the first person plural. This is why a verb is always conjugated by saying *I* first, *you* second and *he/she/it* third (or *we, you* and *they*).
- Draw the chart below on the board, but without the pronouns. Add the pronouns to the board as you talk about them:

	Singular	Plural
First person	I	we
Second Person	you	you
Third person	he/she/it	they

- Remind the children that the form the verb takes depends on which pronoun is being used. Conjugate *to like*, using the pronoun actions, and point out that the verb form is different in the third person singular: instead of *like*, the verb changes to *likes*.
- Now say *Jane likes* and ask the children whether this is in the first, second or third person. Though there is no pronoun, the children may be able to tell that it is in the third person singular because of the verb form *likes*. However, if it were in the past

1st, 2nd and 3rd Person Singular and Plural

tense, *Jane liked*, they would not be able to tell just from looking at the verb. Instead they would have to think about which pronoun would replace *Jane*: *Jane* is singular and refers to someone else, so *she* would be used. This means it is in the third person singular.

Activity Page
- The children identify the verb and pronoun in each sentence, and underline them in red and pink.
- They then decide whether they are in the first, second or third person singular or plural (*We went*: 1st, plural; *He is*: 3rd, singular; *They launched*: 3rd, plural; *I play*: 1st, singular; *She felt*: 3rd, singular; *It was*: 3rd, singular; *You are*: 2nd, plural; *You painted*: 2nd, singular).
- Finally, the children must decide which pronoun replaces the subject to find the correct answer (*Granny knitted*: 3rd, singular; *gymnasts won*: 3rd, plural; *worm wriggled*: 3rd, singular; *experts valued*: 3rd, plural; *Zack ate*: 3rd, singular).

Extension Activity
- The children rewrite some of the sentences in a different person. They then swap sentences, and identify which person each sentence is in.

Rounding Off
- Go over the children's work, checking their answers.

Spelling: Schwa ‹el›

Spelling Test
- The children turn to the backs of their books and find the column labelled *Spelling Test 22*.
- Call out the spelling words learnt last week.

Revision
- Revise the schwa, which is a swallowed vowel sound that often appears in unstressed syllables. The schwa is the most common vowel sound in English and it makes spelling words tricky as it can be the sound of any swallowed vowel.
- Write these words on the board and identify the schwa in each one: *past**a**, carr**o**t, fung**u**s, orch**a**rd, err**o**r, mann**e**rs*. Blend and sound out the words with the class, saying the schwas in their pure form to help remember the spelling.

Spelling Point
- Remind the children that when multisyllabic words end in /ool/, this unstressed syllable can be spelt several ways: ‹le›, ‹al›, ‹el› and ‹il›. This is because the vowel sound is a schwa. There is no rule for which one should be used, so spellings have to be learnt.
- Remind the children that 'saying it as it sounds' is a useful spelling strategy, which will help them to remember these spellings if they stress the pure form of the schwa when learning the words.

Spelling List
- Read the spelling words with the children and ask them to find and highlight the ‹el› spelling in each word. Remind them that, like other vowels, the 'magic' of the schwa in ‹el› can change a short stressed vowel in the previous syllable into the long vowel sound, as in *s**e**quel* and *y**o**del*, but not in *tunnel, barrel* and *mussel* where the double consonant blocks the influence of the schwa.
- Notice, however, that some words, such as *level, novel, camel* and *travel,* keep their short vowel sound even when there is no consonant doubling (the letter ‹v› is never doubled in English).
- Point out the ‹ow› spelling in *vowel* and *towel,* the soft ‹c› in *cancel,* the ‹k› and ‹ck› spellings of /c/ in *snorkel* and *cockerel,* and the schwa in *cockerel.*
- It is a good idea to blend and sound out the spelling words quickly every day with the children, emphasising the /e/ in ‹el› to help remember the spelling.

level
vowel
novel
camel
model
marvel
tunnel
barrel
travel
towel
cancel
mussel
morsel
snorkel
sequel
yodel
cockerel
scoundrel

Activity Page
- The children look at the misspelt words from the spelling list and write the correct spellings underneath. They then complete each sentence by writing the correct spelling of the missing homophone (*its, its, it's, It's*).
- Finally, they parse the sentence, identify the subject (*scoundrel*) and choose the correct tense (simple present).

In the novel, a cruel scoundrel travels through a long, dark tunnel.

Dictation
- Dictate the following sentences:

1. The author wrote a sequel to her novel.
2. "I kept a travel journal in Brazil," said Rachel.
3. We covered the path with gravel.

Extension Activity
- Write these sentences on the board: *There was bad news in the letter. My aunt is a good storyteller. We are expecting bad weather tomorrow. They had a good time at the party.*
- The children find the adjective *good* or *bad* in each sentence and underline it in blue.
- They then rewrite the sentence twice, first with its comparative and then with its superlative. Remind the class to use *the* with the superlative.

Grammar: Changing Grammatical Person

Aim
• Reinforce the children's ability to identify the first, second and third person. Develop their understanding that when the person is changed, the verb and the rest of the sentence must agree.

Introduction
• Remind the children that a sentence can be written in the first, second or third person and that the person can be singular or plural.
• If you are talking about yourself in the sentence, it is written in the first person and uses the pronoun *I* for the singular and *we* for the plural.
• If you are addressing someone else in the sentence, it is written in the second person and uses the pronoun *you* for both singular and plural.
• If you are talking about someone else in the sentence, it is written in the third person and uses the pronoun *he/she/it* for the singular and *they* for the plural.
• With the class, conjugate the verb *to be* in the simple present and past tenses, doing the pronoun actions.

Main Point
• Write *I went to the library* on the board and ask the children which person it is written in (first person singular). Ask them which pronoun is used for second person singular and write *You went to the library* on the board. Now ask them how they would write the sentence in the third person singular and write *He/She/It went to the library*.
• Now write *I am in the football team* on the board. Ask what would happen if you changed it from the first person to the second person singular. Now write *You are in the football team* on the board and point out that as well as changing *I* to *you*, the verb *to be* has also changed from *am* to *are*. This is because *I* and *you* are the subject of the sentence and the verb and subject must always agree.
• Continue to change the person in this sentence, asking the children which pronoun/verb form each one should take. Remind the children that they may need to change more than the subject and verb for the rest of the sentence to agree.
• Write *I am riding my new bike* on the board. Ask the children what would happen if the sentence was written from a different point of view: if it was describing a boy riding a bike, for example.
• Write *He is riding my new bike* and ask the children whether this sounds right. While it is grammatically correct, the bike still belongs to me, the first person; *my* should be changed to *his*: *He is riding **his** new bike*. Continue to change the person, as before, discussing which personal pronoun, verb form and possessive adjective is needed each time.

Activity Page
• In each sentence, the children underline the verb in red and the pronoun in pink. They then decide whether they are in the first, second or third person singular or plural (*He listens*: 3rd, singular; *I descended*: 1st, singular; *It is*: 3rd, singular; *She will be visiting*: 3rd, singular; *You are wearing*: 2nd, singular; *We are going*: 1st, plural; *They were sitting*: 3rd, plural; *You will do*: 2nd, plural).
• Finally, they rewrite the sentences, changing the person as instructed (1st person plural: *We descended*; 3rd person plural: *They are*; 2nd person plural: *You will be visiting*; 3rd person singular: *He/She is wearing*; 3rd person plural: *They are going*; 3rd person singular: *He/She/It was sitting*; 2nd person singular: *You will do... yourself*). In the last sentence, the children must remember to make the rest of the sentence agree, changing *yourselves* to *yourself*.

Extension Activity
• The children write a couple of sentences in the first person singular about something they have done recently. They then rewrite the sentences in the third person singular and in the third person plural, as if other people were doing it.

Rounding Off
• Go over the children's work, checking their answers.

77

Spelling: Schwa ‹il›

Spelling Test
- The children turn to the backs of their books and find the column labelled *Spelling Test 23.*
- Call out the spelling words learnt last week.

Revision
- Revise the schwa, which is a swallowed vowel sound that often appears in unstressed syllables. The schwa is the most common vowel sound in English and it can be the sound of any swallowed vowel.
- Write these words on the board and identify the schwa in each one: *private, method, focus, coward, mirror, interest.* Blend and sound out the words with the class, saying the schwas in their pure form to help remember the spelling.

Spelling Point
- Remind the children that when multisyllabic words end in /ool/, this unstressed syllable can be spelt several ways: ‹le›, ‹al›, ‹el› and ‹il›. This is because the vowel sound is a schwa. There is no rule for which one should be used and so the spellings have to be learnt. Remind the children that 'saying it as it sounds' is a useful spelling strategy, which will help them to remember these spellings if they stress the pure form of the schwa when learning the words.

Spelling List
- Read the spelling words with the children and ask them to highlight the ‹il› spelling in each word.
- Remind them that, like other vowels, the 'magic' of the schwa in ‹il› can change a short stressed vowel in the previous syllable into the long vowel sound, as in *pupil* and *evil*, but not in *fossil* where the double consonant blocks the influence of the schwa.
- Notice, however, that some words, such as *civil, peril* and *basil,* keep their short vowel sound even when there is no consonant doubling.
- Point out the soft ‹c› in *civil, pencil, council* and *stencil* and the soft ‹g› in *gerbil,* the capital in the proper noun *April,* and the ‹qu› in *tranquil.*

civil
pupil
pencil
weevil
evil
peril
nostril
basil
April
fossil
gerbil
anvil
utensil
tendril
lentil
council
stencil
tranquil

Activity Page
- The children unscramble the letters and add them to ‹il› to make the words (*pencil, pupil, weevil, lentil, fossil, gerbil, utensil, stencil, nostril, basil, anvil, tendril, peril, civil, tranquil, council*).

- The children then add the punctuation to the sentences: 1. *"Can I borrow your pencil?" asked the journalist.* 2. *The actor exclaimed, "You scoundrel!"* 3. *Parsley, basil, mint and rosemary are types of herb.* 4. *What is the final total?*
- Then they write the correct personal pronoun(s) for each grammatical person: *I, you, he/she/it, we, you, they.* Finally, they parse the sentence, identify the subject (*pupil*) and choose the correct tense, (present continuous).

The pupil is drawing carefully inside the stencil with a green pencil.

Dictation
- Dictate the following sentences:

1. The scientists examined a massive fossil.
2. April drew an evil weevil.
3. We took our gerbil to the animal hospital.

Extension Activity
- Write the sentences on the board, drawing boxes where punctuation marks should be: 1. *Ben's house is in London but his twin cousins' family live in Scotland.* 2. *"Can I have a pet gerbil?" the daughter asked her dad.* 3. *"What a marvel!" gasped Great Aunt Ivy.* 4. *The children's new beds arrived this morning.*
- The children write the sentences, adding in the punctuation marks

Grammar: Parsing Verbs

Aim
- Introduce the idea of parsing a verb: this is where the children have to decide whether a verb is singular or plural, in the first, second or third person, and in the simple or continuous tense, past, present or future.

Introduction
- Revise the first, second and third person, which can be singular or plural. Remind the children that if they are talking about themselves in a sentence, they are writing in the first person and should use *I* or *we*. If they are addressing someone else, they are writing in the second person and should use *you*. If they are talking about someone else, they are writing in the third person and should use either *he*, *she* or *it* for the singular and *they* for the plural.
- Revise the irregular past and present simple tenses of the verb *to be*: write *I am*, *it is*, *they are*, *she was* and *we were* on the board. Ask whether each one is in the past or present tense and whether the tense is simple or continuous. Then discuss whether the verb is in the first, second or third person, singular or plural.

Main Point
- Remind the children that when they parse a sentence, they must analyse all the words; they should look at the function of each word to decide which part of speech it is.
- Explain that they can do something similar to a verb in a sentence: they can decide when it happened (the past, present or future) and what tense it is in (simple or continuous). Then, by looking at the subject, they can decide if the verb is in first, second or third person and whether it is singular or plural.
- Write *She arranges the flowers very artistically* on the board. Ask the children to identify the verb (*arranges*) and subject (*She*). Remind them that the subject is the noun or pronoun that does the verb action, so they should ask *Who (or what) arranges the flowers?* to find the subject. Underline *arranges* in red and draw a box around *She*, putting a small ‹s› in the corner. Now the children can parse the verb.
- Draw four simple beehives on the board. Write the words *singular* and *plural* in the first one. Discuss whether the pronoun *She* is singular or plural and circle *singular*.
- Then write *first person*, *second person* and *third person* in the second beehive. Ask the children which person to circle for *She arranges* (third person).
- Move on to the next hive, writing *past*, *present* and *future* inside. Discuss when the verb *arranges* is happening and circle *present*.
- Finally, write *simple* and *continuous* in the last

beehive. Look at how the verb (*arranges*) is formed: it does not use the auxiliary verb *to be* with the present participle (e.g. *is arranging*), so it is not the continuous tense. Instead it has the suffix ‹-s› for the third person singular, so it must be the simple tense.

Activity Page
- The children identify the verb and subject in each sentence. They then parse the verb (*She will cook*: singular, 3rd, future, simple; *I explored*: singular, 1st, past, simple; *He travels*: singular, 3rd, present, simple; *camel was eating*: singular, 3rd, past, continuous; *We were washing*: plural, 1st, past, continuous; *Zack sorted*: singular, 3rd, past, simple; *They will cancel*: plural, 3rd, future, simple; *I am wrestling*: singular, 1st, present, continuous; *You yodel*: plural, 2nd, present, simple; *climbers are ascending*: plural, 3rd, present, continuous; *We will be roasting*: plural, 1st, future, continuous).
- Explain that when parsing a verb in the second person (you), they will need to look for extra information to work out if it is singular or plural. In the ninth sentence, the word *together* shows there is more than one person.

Extension Activity
- Write more sentences on the board for the children to parse. You could use some from the activity page, changing the person and/or tense each time.

Spelling: ‹-ery›

Spelling Test
- The children turn to the backs of their books and find the column labelled *Spelling Test 24*.
- Call out the spelling words learnt last week.

Revision
- Revise the schwa, which makes spelling words tricky as it can be the sound of any swallowed vowel.
- Write these /ool/ words on the board and identify the spelling for each one: *April, level, several, tranquil, tunnel, plural*. Blend and sound out the words with the class, saying the schwas in their pure form to help remember the spelling.

Spelling Point
- Introduce the suffix ‹-ery›, which makes nouns that can mean: a place for a business or activity (e.g. *bakery* and *nursery*); a type or collection (e.g. *confectionery*); a practice or occupation (e.g. *archery* and *butchery*); a quality or characteristic (e.g. *bravery*); or a state or condition (e.g. *slavery*).
- Write the spelling words on the board and identify the stress in each one. Point out that the last syllable, ‹ery›, is unstressed and the vowel is a schwa.
- Explain that not all ‹ery› words use the suffix: *every* and *very* are not nouns and simply happen to be spelt this way; words like *flowery* are adjectives made by adding ‹-y› to the noun.

Spelling List
- Read the spelling words with the children and ask them to highlight the ‹ery› spellings. Remind them that, like other vowels, the 'magic' of the schwa can change a short stressed vowel in the previous syllable into the long vowel sound, as in *bravery, slavery, scenery* and *bakery*, but not in *gallery, pottery, lottery* and *skulduggery*, where the double consonant blocks the influence of the schwa.
- Notice, however, that the words *delivery* and *discovery* keep their short vowel sound even though there is no consonant doubling, as the letter ‹v› is never doubled in English.
- Point out the ‹tch› in *butchery*, the silent letter digraph ‹sc› in *scenery*, the soft ‹g› in *imagery* and *surgery*, the ‹k› in *bakery* and *skulduggery*, the ‹ur› spelling of /ir/ in *surgery* and *nursery*, the ‹o› saying /u/ in *discovery*, the ‹ea› saying /e/ in *treachery*, and the ‹tion› in *stationery* and *confectionery*.

gallery
pottery
archery
lottery
bravery
slavery
butchery
scenery
bakery
delivery
imagery
discovery
surgery
nursery
treachery
stationery
confectionery
skulduggery

Activity Page
- The children write in the spelling word that completes each sentence (*nursery, bravery, bakery, discovery, pottery, surgery, gallery, delivery, stationery, scenery, archery, treachery*).
- They then make nouns ending in ‹-ery› from the root words, using the spelling rules which apply when a suffix begins with a vowel (*bravery, pottery, lottery, bakery, scenery, imagery, delivery, surgery, nursery, treachery*).
- Finally, they parse the sentence, identify the subject (*We*) and then parse the verb (1st person plural, simple past). *Bakery* is a noun acting as an adjective.
We looked hungrily at the confectionery in the bakery window.

Dictation
- Dictate the following sentences:

1. The visitors liked the pottery in the gallery.
2. "Did you cancel the delivery?" asked Jim.
3. They keep barrels of flour at the bakery.

Extension Activity
- Write the following job titles on the board: *baker, butcher, florist, confectioner, grocer, stationer, jeweller, tailor*. The children write a list of things that they could buy from each person, using the listing comma correctly.

Grammar: Questions and Statements

Aim
- Refine the children's understanding of a sentence and develop their ability to tell the difference between a statement and a question.

Introduction
- Revise sentences. Remind the children that all sentences must make sense, start with a capital letter, contain a verb and subject, and end with a full stop, question mark or exclamation mark.
- Write on the board *she went to hairdressers*. Ask the children what is needed to make it a proper sentence. Make the corrections on the board: *She went to **the** hairdressers.*
- Now write *The exciting festival* on the board, add a full stop, and ask if this is enough to make it a sentence.
- Point out to the children that although the words make sense, there is no verb and therefore no subject, so it is not a sentence but a phrase.
- Write some more phrases on the board and turn them into sentences with the children.

Main Point
- Now write on the board *When is the exciting festival?* Ask the children what is different about this sentence and why (it is a question because it starts with the question word *when* and ends in a question mark).
- Remind the children that they know seven ‹wh› question words; *what, why, when, where, who, which, whose*. These words can be used at the beginning of a sentence to get new information.
- Ask the children to suggest some questions, using the question words.
- Write some on the board, reminding them to finish with a question mark.
- Now write *The festival is exciting*. Ask the children to make it into a question: *Is the festival exciting?*
- Discuss what is different here: a question mark has been added as usual, but instead of using a question word, the word *is* has been moved to the front of the sentence.
- Explain that when the main verb in a sentence is *to be*, it can be made into a question by moving the verb to the beginning of the sentence.
- Ask the children to think of some more examples.
- Remind the children that they have learnt three types of sentence so far: ones that ask for more information and end in ‹?› (questions), ones that express something very strongly and end in ‹!› (exclamations), and ones that state information and end in a full stop (statements).

Activity Page
- The children decide whether each sentence is a statement or a question, put a circle around the question words, and add the correct punctuation: question (*who*); statement; question (*which*); statement; statement; question (*where*); question (*when*); statement; question (*why*); question (*what*); question (*whose*).
- They then do the same for the sentences at the bottom of the sheet, but instead of looking for question words, they underline the form of the verb *to be* in red. If the form of *to be* is at the beginning of the sentence, the sentence is a question and needs a question mark: question (*Am*), statement (*were*), question (*Are*), statement (*was*), question (*Is*), statement (*are*), statement (*was*), question (*Were*).

Extension Activity
- The children use words from this week's spelling list to write questions that begin with either a question word or *to be* as the main verb. They then work in pairs, swapping questions and turning them into statements.

Rounding Off
- Go over the activity page with the children, checking their answers. If they have done the extension activity, ask some of them to read their questions and statements.

Spelling: ‹-ary›

Spelling Test
- The children turn to the backs of their books and find the column labelled *Spelling Test 25*.
- Call out the spelling words learnt last week.

Revision
- Revise the schwa, the most common vowel sound in English, which makes spelling words tricky as it can be the sound of any swallowed vowel.
- Write these /ool/ words on the board and identify the spelling for each one: *hospital, novel, pencil, total, travel, pupil*. Blend and sound out the words with the class, saying the schwas in their pure form to help remember the spelling.

Spelling Point
- Introduce the suffix ‹-ary›, which can make nouns or adjectives that mean *connected with*. Some ‹ary› nouns refer to places or things where something is kept, as in *diary, library, glossary* and *dictionary*.
- Write some spelling words on the board, say them with the class and identify where the stress is.
- Point out that the last syllable, ‹ary›, is unstressed and the vowel is a schwa. This makes it difficult to hear the difference between words that end in ‹ery› and ‹ary›, and the spellings have to be learnt.
- Remind the children that if they are unsure of a spelling, they should look it up in a dictionary.

Spelling List
- Read the spelling words with the children and ask them to find and highlight the ‹ary› spelling in each word.
- Remind them that, like other vowels, the 'magic' of the schwa in ‹ary› can change a short stressed vowel in the previous syllable into the long vowel sound, as in *primary, diary* and *vocabulary*, but not in *glossary* and *necessary*, where the double consonant blocks the influence of the schwa.
- Point out the influence from other 'magic' vowels, as in *vocabulary, itinerary* and *evolutionary*, the ‹i› saying /ie/ in *library*, the soft ‹c› and ‹g› in *necessary* and *imaginary*, the ‹tion› in *dictionary* and *evolutionary*, and the double consonants ‹nn› in *anniversary*.

literary
primary
solitary
diary
library
glossary
ordinary
necessary
imaginary
dictionary
temporary
vocabulary
itinerary
secretary
hereditary
anniversary
evolutionary
complementary

Activity Page
- The children look again at the spelling words and

sort them into alphabetical order (*anniversary, complementary, diary, dictionary, evolutionary, glossary, hereditary, imaginary, itinerary, library, literary, necessary, ordinary, primary, secretary, solitary, temporary, vocabulary*).
- The children then look up the word *apothecary* in the dictionary and see how many other words they can make using its letters.
- Next, they write in the correct homophones to correct the sentences (*It's, it's, its, its, its*). Finally, they parse the sentence, identify the subject (*boy*) and then parse the verb (3rd person singular, simple present). The <u>boy</u> <u>in</u> the <u>library</u> <u>has</u> a <u>huge</u> <u>vocabulary</u>.

Dictation
- Dictate the following sentences:

1. I found a dictionary in the public library.
2. Is the glossary in alphabetical order?
3. "Here is your itinerary," said the secretary.

Extension Activity
- Write the sentences on the board, leaving gaps for *its* and *it's*: *The hospital is celebrating [its] fiftieth anniversary. Do you want me to check the date for the party? I think [it's] written in my diary. "[It's] so tranquil here," sighed the visitor. The pottery has reduced [its] prices on all [its] most expensive items.*
- The children complete the sentences.

Grammar: Changing a Statement into a Question

Aim
- Develop the children's ability to turn statements into questions by moving the auxiliary verb to the beginning of the sentence.

Introduction
- Revise the three types of sentence that the children have learnt so far: statements give some information and end in a full stop; questions ask for more information and end in a question mark; and exclamations express something very strongly and end in an exclamation mark.
- Remind the children that as well as ending in the correct punctuation, all sentences must make sense, start with a capital letter and contain a verb and subject. (If the words make sense but there is no verb, it is called a phrase.)
- Discuss the ways the children know to turn a statement into a question: for example, they could use one of the ‹wh› question words: *what, why, when, where, who, which, whose.*
- Write *We will go in the tunnel* and ask the children to use some of the ‹wh› words to ask for more information. They could ask: *Who will go in the tunnel? Why will they go in the tunnel? When will they go in the tunnel? Which tunnel will they go in? Where will the tunnel be?*
- Asking themselves such questions can help the children when they are writing stories.

Main Point
- Remind the children that they know another way to change a statement into a question.
- Write *They are in the tunnel*. Point out that it can be turned into a question by moving *are* to the beginning of the sentence and replacing the full stop with a question mark, so it reads *Are they in the tunnel?*
- Explain that the children can make a question in a similar way with statements that have auxiliary verbs.
- Look at the original statement *We will go in the tunnel* and ask the children to identify the verb (*will go*).
- To make it a question, the auxiliary verb (*will*) is moved to the beginning of the sentence; however, the main part of the verb, *go*, stays where it is. The resulting question reads *Will we go in the tunnel?*
- Write some more statements that contain auxiliary verbs on the board and turn them into questions with the class. Possible auxiliary verbs include: *has, had, have, can, may, could, should, would, must, might, did, does.*

Changing a Statement into a Question

If you want to change a statement into a question and it has an auxiliary verb and a main verb, you only move the auxiliary verb to the beginning of the sentence. Rewrite these statements as questions by moving the auxiliary verb in bold.

The tent **has** split down the side.

Has the tent split down the side?

Adjectives **can** describe nouns.

I **may** buy some flowers today.

She **had** read many classic novels.

The crumbs **have** fallen on the floor.

A castle **should** have huge stone walls.

We **must** finish our homework tonight.

It **would** be nice to live in a palace.

The play **could** be more dramatic.

He **does** like chocolate ice cream.

The blackbird **was** looking for earthworms.

They **might** have chocolate cake at the party.

You **did** get jostled in all the hustle and bustle.

53

Activity Page
- The children write the statements as questions. Remind them that to do this, they should move the auxiliary verb in bold to the beginning of the sentence and replace the full stop with a question mark (*Can adjectives describe..? May I buy..? Had she read..? Have the crumbs fallen..? Should a castle have..? Must we finish..? Would it be..? Could the play be..? Does he like..? Was the blackbird looking..? Might they have..? Did you get..?*).

Extension Activity
- The children use words from this week's spelling list, or perhaps from a topic they are studying, to write some statements using auxiliary verbs.
- They then make each statement into a question by moving the auxiliary verb to the beginning and replacing the full stop with a question mark.

Rounding Off
- Go over the activity page with the children, checking their answers. If they have done the extension activity, ask some of them to read their statements and questions.

83

Spelling: ‹-ory›

Spelling Test
- The children turn to the backs of their books and find the column labelled *Spelling Test 26*.
- In any order, call out the spelling words learnt last week. The children write the words on the lines.

Revision
- Revise the suffixes ‹-ery› and ‹-ary›.
- Write these words on the board and identify the spellings: *butchery, scenery, diary, library, stationery, ordinary*. Look at other spelling features in the words and stress the pure vowel sound in ‹ery› and ‹ary› to help remember the spelling.

Spelling Point
- Introduce the suffix ‹-ory›, which can make adjectives and nouns that relate to the root word; so if something is *compulsory*, you are compelled (forced) to do it, and a *directory* directs you to what you are looking for. Some ‹ory› nouns refer to places with a particular use, as in *factory* and *dormitory*.
- Write some spelling words on the board, say them with the class and identify where the stress is.
- Point out that, apart from the monosyllabic (and therefore stressed) word *story*, the last syllable, ‹ory›, is unstressed and the vowel is a schwa. This makes it difficult to hear the difference between words that end in ‹ery›, ‹ary› and ‹ory›, and the spellings have to be learnt.
- Remind the children that if they are unsure of how to spell a word, they should look it up in a dictionary.

Spelling List
- Read the spelling words with the children, go over the meaning of any words they may not know, and ask them to find and highlight the ‹ory› spelling in each word.
- Remind them that, like other vowels, the 'magic' of the schwa in ‹ory› can change a short stressed vowel in the previous syllable into the long vowel sound, as in *theory* and *contributory*, but not in *accessory*, where the double consonant blocks the influence of the schwa.
- Point out any schwas, as in *inventory* and *introductory*, and the ‹cc› saying /ks/ in *accessory*.
- It is a good idea to blend and sound out the spelling words quickly every day with the children, emphasising the /o/ in ‹ory› to help remember the spelling.

story
history
victory
factory
theory
territory
category
directory
inventory
accessory
dormitory
compulsory
preparatory
satisfactory
laboratory
observatory
introductory
contributory

Activity Page
- The children unscramble the letters in the test tubes and add them to ‹ory› to make words from the spelling list (*theory, observatory, satisfactory, story, dormitory, territory, victory, compulsory, accessory, history, factory, category*). They then combine the root words with the prefixes and suffixes to make new words (*review, misquoted, irreplaceable*).
- Each child then puts his or her first initial in the box and writes a word beginning with that letter for each of the categories.
- Finally, they parse the sentence, identify the subject (*You*) and then parse the verb (2nd person singular or plural, future continuous). *Your* is a possessive adjective describing who the homework belongs to. *History* is a noun acting as an adjective and should be underlined in blue.

You will be writing a story for your history homework.

Dictation
- Dictate the following sentences:

1. The factory makes exclusive travel accessories.
2. I read the introductory chapter of the history book.
3. The story has a very unsatisfactory ending.

Extension Activity
- The children see how many words they can make using the letters in *unsatisfactory*.

Grammar: Simple and Compound Sentences

Aim
- Introduce the idea that a sentence with a subject and verb is called a simple sentence. When two simple sentences are joined together with one of the following conjunctions, it is called a compound sentence: *for, and, nor, but, or, yet* or *so* (FANBOYS).

Introduction
- Revise conjunctions, which are the (usually) small words that join parts of a sentence together, such as *and* and *or*.
- Ask the children to think of other conjunctions, (e.g. *because, but, so, while*), write them on the board and underline them in purple. Say them again, doing the action for conjunctions (the children hold their hands apart with their palms facing up. Then they move their hands together, so one is on top of the other.)
- Now ask the children how to identify a sentence: it must make sense, start with a capital letter, contain a verb and subject, and end with a full stop (statement), question mark (question) or exclamation mark (exclamation).
- Ask the children what words are called when they make sense but do not have a verb and subject (a phrase).
- Write some short sentences, phrases, incomplete or unpunctuated sentences, and words making no sense on the board. Discuss them with the children: *we went to the park* (sentence not punctuated correctly: *We went to the park.*); *He stopped.* (short, but still a sentence); *ladybird, beetle, bee and flea* (phrase); *She was frightened of.* (incomplete sentence); *Rubble trouble flicked Mick.* (makes no sense); *She sang untunefully.* (sentence).

Main Point
- Write on the board: *I went to my friend's house. We played games.* Tell the children that this sounds a bit stilted and that sometimes it is better to have a longer, more flowing sentence than two short ones.
- Ask the children how they could join the two sentences together: the simplest way is to use the conjunction *and*. Add *and* to the board, and then remove the full stop at the end of the first sentence and the capital letter at the start of the second one: *I went to my friend's house and we played games.*
- Remind the children that when two words are joined together to make a new word, it is called a compound word. Explain that when two or more sentences are joined together with a conjunction, it is called a compound sentence, and the two original sentences are called simple sentences.
- A simple sentence expresses a complete thought and only has one verb-subject relationship. A compound

sentence will always have two or more verb-subject relationships separated by a conjunction.
- Underline *and* in purple. Ask the children to identify the verbs (*went* and *played*) and subjects (*I* and *we*) either side of *and* in the sentence. Explain that if a sentence has a conjunction but does not have more than one verb and subject (as in *We went home and played games* or *I went to the park and the swimming pool*), it is not a compound sentence.
- Later on, the children can learn that conjunctions used to join compound sentences are called co-ordinating conjunctions.

Activity Page
- The children write inside the outlined word *Conjunctions* and the outlined conjunctions, using a purple pencil.
- They then write compound sentences by joining the pairs of simple sentences with the conjunction shown in bold, underlining it in purple.
- Finally, they identify the conjunction in each compound sentence and underline it in purple (*and, yet, but*). Then they write down the remaining words as two simple sentences, using the correct punctuation, making sure both have a subject and verb.

Extension Activity
- Write more pairs of simple sentences on the board. The children make them into compound sentences.

Spelling: ‹-ant›

Spelling Test
- The children turn to the backs of their books and find the column labelled *Spelling Test 27*.
- Call out the spelling words learnt last week.

Revision
- Revise the suffixes ‹-ery›, ‹-ary› and ‹-ory›.
- Write these words on the board and identify the spellings: *the**ory**, brav**ery**, necess**ary**, surg**ery**, imagin**ary**, hist**ory***. Look at other spelling features in the words and stress the pure vowel sound in ‹ery›, ‹ary› and ‹ory› to help remember the spelling.

Spelling Point
- Introduce the suffix ‹-ant›. This can make adjectives meaning *having the quality or characteristic of* the root word. For example, if you find something *pleasant*, it pleases you, and if winners are *triumphant*, they celebrate their triumph. The suffix can also make nouns that do the action of the root word, or help make it happen, as in *servant, merchant* and *participant*.
- Write some spelling words on the board, say them with the class and identify where the stress is.
- Point out that, apart from the monosyllabic (and therefore stressed) word *scant*, the last syllable, ‹ant›, is unstressed and the vowel is a schwa.
- Remind the children that if they are unsure of how to spell a word, they should consult a dictionary.

Spelling List
- Read the spelling words with the children and ask them to highlight the ‹ant› spelling in each word.
- Point out that, like other vowels, the 'magic' of the schwa in ‹ant› makes the first ‹a› say /ai/ in *vacant*.
- Point out any other schwas, such as in *rel**e**vant, brilli**a**nt* and *extrav**a**gant*, the ‹ea› saying /e/ in *pleasant*, the ‹au› spelling in *restaurant* (and how the second ‹a› can be said with either a schwa or as /o/), the soft ‹c› in *participant*, the ‹ph› saying /f/ and the 'magic' from the ‹u› making the ‹i› say /ie/ in *triumphant*, and the ‹oy› spelling in *flamboyant*.
- It is a good idea to blend and sound out the spelling words every day, emphasising the /a/ in ‹ant› to help remember the spelling.

scant
distant
servant
important
vacant
instant
relevant
merchant
brilliant
reluctant
pleasant
restaurant
extravagant
participant
valiant
triumphant
insignificant
flamboyant

Activity Page
- The children write a sentence for each of the listed

spelling words. They then look at the word in each mirror and think of a word that means the opposite (possible answers are: *vacant: occupied, distant: close, important: unimportant, pleasant: unpleasant, brilliant: dull, reluctant: eager, insignificant: significant, relevant: irrelevant*).
- Finally, they parse the sentence, identify the subject (*We*) and then parse the verb (1st person plural, past continuous). *Chinese* is a proper adjective and needs a capital letter.

We were enjoying a pleasant dinner at a Chinese restaurant.

Dictation
- Dictate the following sentences:

1. The valiant knights were triumphant in battle.
2. "It's a truly fragrant rice," the merchant said.
3. The laboratory assistant made a scientific discovery.

Extension Activity
- Write these pairs of sentences on the board: 1. *It was very muddy. We had a brilliant time.* 2. *We could eat at home. We could go to a restaurant.* 3. *It is a pleasant day. I do not want to go out.* 4. *They went for a walk. They had a picnic.* 5. *It was raining outside. We took an umbrella.*
- The children join each pair of sentences with a conjunction to make a compound sentence.

Grammar: More Homophone Mix-Ups (1)

Aim
- Reinforce the children's understanding of homophones and develop their ability to choose between similar-sounding words in their writing.

Introduction
- Revise the homophones that the children know so far: *our* and *are*; *their*, *there* and *they're*; *your* and *you're*; *its* and *it's*; *to*, *two* and *too*; and *where*, *wear* and *were*. *Our* is more properly pronounced /ou-r/ but in practice it is often pronounced /ar/ and can be confused with *are*. *Were* is not strictly a homophone of *where*, but their spellings are often confused so it helps to look at them together.
- Point out that *are* and *were* are parts of the verb *to be*. Also point out that some of the homophones are possessive adjectives (*our, your, their, its*), while others are contractions (*they're, you're, it's*).
- Children often find *its* and *it's* particularly difficult because apostrophe ‹s› can also be used to show possession; however, it is only used in this way to make possessive nouns and not possessive adjectives, and *its* is a possessive adjective.
- Remind the children that it is important to be careful when writing homophones; if the wrong one is used, their writing will not make sense.

Main Point
- Ask the children if they can think of any other homophones. Write their suggestions on the board, discussing the spellings and meanings. Add the words from the activity page, look at the spellings, and check that the children know what they mean.
- If the children are unsure of a word, ask them to look it up in the dictionary. See who can find it first.
- Remind the children that they need to stop and think before writing a homophone, decide which meaning is needed, and think how the word with that meaning is spelt.
- Using the information they already know can sometimes help the children remember different spellings and meanings. For example, *bridal* is an adjective made by adding ‹-al› to the root word *bride*, whereas *bridle* means the straps that go on a horse's head when it is ridden. If the sentence requires the adjective, the children can remember to use the ‹-al› spelling.
- They should also be able to work out when to use *days* rather than *daze*; they know that ‹s› is added to nouns to make them plural, and that the ‹ay› spelling of /ai/ is usually used at the end of a word.
- Similarly, they know that ‹-ed› can be added to a verb to make the simple past tense, and that it can be pronounced /d/ (as in *sailed*), /id/ (as in *sorted*) or /t/

Homophone Mix-ups

Check the meanings of these homophones in a dictionary and use each one in a sentence.

bridal / bridle / flew / flu / flue / you / ewe / yew / days / daze / herd / heard / rest / wrest / genes / jeans / guessed / guest

57

(as in *guessed*). They also know that the consonant is often doubled before adding ‹-ed›, so if a sentence needs the past tense of the verb, the children can be confident that it is *guessed* rather than *guest*.
- Ask the children to think of sentences for some of the homophones and discuss which spellings they would use.

Activity Page
- The children write a sentence for each homophone, using the correct meaning and spelling. If the children are unsure of any words, they can use a dictionary to look up them up.

Extension Activity
- Write the main homophones learnt so far on the board: *our* and *are*; *their*, *there* and *they're*; *your* and *you're*; *its* and *it's*; *to*, *two* and *too*; and *where*, *wear* and *were*. Extra homophones could also be added (e.g. *you, ewe* and *yew*; *mail* and *male*; *thyme* and *time*; *hair* and *hare*; *right* and *write*; *would* and *wood*; *muscle* and *mussel*).
- Working in pairs, the children take turns to dictate sentences that contain the homophones to each other. Then, together, they check whether the correct spellings have been used.

Rounding Off
- Go over the children's work, checking their answers.

Spelling: ‹-ent›

Spelling Test
- The children turn to the backs of their books and find the column labelled *Spelling Test 28*.
- Call out the spelling words learnt last week.

Revision
- Revise the suffixes ‹-ery›, ‹-ary›, ‹-ory› and ‹-ant›.
- Write these words on the board and identify the spellings: *lottery, dictionary, merchant, literary, accessory, distant*.
- Look at other spelling features in the words and stress the pure vowel sound in ‹ery›, ‹ary›, ‹ory› and ‹ant› to help remember the spelling.

Spelling Point
- Introduce the suffix ‹-ent›, which is found in nouns and adjectives of Latin origin. Nouns with this suffix usually do the action of the root word, as in *student* and *president*. However, there is often an ‹m› in front, making ‹-ment›; these nouns give the result of the root word, as in *treatment* and *argument*. (If you treat someone, you give them treatment and if you argue, you have an argument.)
- Write some spelling words on the board, say them with the class and identify where the stress is.
- Point out that the last syllable, ‹ent›, is unstressed and the vowel is a schwa; the only exceptions are *spent* and *event*. This makes it difficult to hear the difference between words that end in ‹ant› and ‹ent›, and the spellings have to be learnt.

Spelling List
- Read the spelling words with the children and ask them to highlight the ‹ent› spelling in each word.
- Remind them that, like other vowels, the 'magic' of the schwa in ‹ent› can change a short stressed vowel in the previous syllable into the long vowel sound, as in *student, moment, affluent* and *argument*.
- Point out the ‹s› saying /z/ in *present* and *president*, the ‹are› spelling of /air/ in *parent*, the ‹o› saying /oo/ and ‹ve› saying /v/ in *movement*, the ‹ff› in *affluent*, the ‹ea› spelling in *treatment*, the prefix in *independent*, the double ‹tt› in *settlement* (which blocks the 'magic' from the schwa in ‹le›) and the silent ‹n› in *government* and *environment*. It is a good idea to go over the spelling words every day, emphasising the /e/ in ‹ent› to help remember the spelling.

event
present
parent
spent
student
moment
movement
affluent
equipment
president
treatment
independent
argument
settlement
experiment
government
environment
development

Activity Page
- The children decide which words from the spelling list the phrases describe (*parent, argument, present, president, independent, affluent, experiment, spent, moment, environment, development, government*).
- They then add the punctuation to the sentences. (1. *"Good evening to mums, dads, brothers and sisters,"* began the student. 2. *The president asked, "Do you have the measurements?"* 3. *"What a lot of equipment!" exclaimed the explorer.*)
- Finally, they parse the sentence, identify the subject (*parents*) and then parse the verb (3rd person plural, simple future).
  The student's parents will attend the school event next week.

Dictation
- Dictate the following sentences:

1. The students spent several hours at the observatory.
2. It is not relevant at the present moment.
3. "We need your parent's agreement," said the teacher

Extension Activity
- Write these homophones on the board: *stationery* and *stationary*, *current* and *currant*, *compliment* and *complement*, *assent* and *ascent*, *descent* and *dissent*.
- The children use a dictionary to find the meanings for the homophones and write them down.

Grammar: Noun Phrases

Aim
- Refine the children's knowledge of nouns by introducing the term *noun phrase*, which is the name for a noun and all the words that describe it.

Introduction
- Briefly revise the types of noun that the children know: proper nouns, which start with a capital letter, are the names given to particular people, places and dates, and common nouns are the names for things that often have *a*, *an* or *the* in front of them. Common nouns can be divided into concrete nouns, abstract nouns and collective nouns.
- The children know that singular nouns can be made possessive by adding apostrophe ‹s›. This is also true for irregular plural nouns that do not end in ‹s› (e.g. *men's*). If a plural ends in ‹s›, the possessive is made by adding just the apostrophe.
- Call out a variety of nouns and ask the children to do the appropriate actions (see Nouns, pages 6 to 7).

Main Point
- Write *A famous artist* on the board and ask the children if it is a sentence. The children should say that it is not a sentence, because although it makes sense, it does not have a verb or subject.
- Ask the children what we call such words (a phrase) and parse it with the children: *a* is the indefinite article used in front of a noun to show that it is singular; *famous* is an adjective used to describe a noun; and *artist* is the noun that the other two words are describing (or modifying).
- Explain that because the phrase is about the noun *artist*, it is called a noun phrase. Underline the noun in black and draw a box around the three words.
- Now ask the children to use the phrase in a sentence (e.g. *A famous artist painted the two black and white pandas*). Point out that this sentence has another noun phrase (*the two black and white pandas*). Underline the word *pandas* in black and draw a box around all the words in the phrase.
- Tell the children that they can check whether they have identified a noun phrase correctly by replacing it with a pronoun: if *A famous artist* is replaced by *He* or *She* and *the black and white pandas* is replaced by *them*, the sentence still makes sense: *She painted them*.
- Explain that not all words in a noun phrase come before the noun. Write *a boy with red hair* and discuss how the other words give more information about the boy, including the second noun *hair*.
- Write *I saw a boy with red hair* and underline *boy* and *hair* and put a black box around the noun phrase. Ask the children whether it would still

make sense if they replaced the phrase with the pronoun *him*. It would then be *I saw him*, so the noun phrase is correct.
- Point out that when the words in a noun phrase come after the noun, there is usually another noun in the phrase.

Activity Page
- The children identify the noun and noun phrase in each sentence (*The hot crusty loaves; A big white goose; The old wooden fence; twelve tiny calves; his new Spanish guitar; the black and white penguins; the dusty, narrow, winding road; That young brown rabbit, the tasty carrot; some curious visitors, the historic house*).
- They then underline the nouns in each noun phrase and decide which phrase is needed to complete each sentence (*a cat up a tree; Some cars on the road; the house next door; The boys at school; the dog with a sore paw; That man under the umbrella; This picture above the fireplace; the fastest horse in the race*). Finally, they write a noun phrase of their own and draw a picture in the frame.

Extension Activity
- Write some nouns on the board and ask the children to use them in a noun phrase. They then write the phrase in a sentence, underlining the noun in black and putting a box around all the words in the phrase.

Spelling: ‹-ist›

Spelling Test
- The children turn to the backs of their books and find the column labelled *Spelling Test 29*.
- Call out the spelling words learnt last week.

Revision
- Revise the suffixes ‹-ery›, ‹-ary›, ‹-ory›, ‹-ant› and ‹-ent›.
- Write these words on the board and identify the spellings: *par**ent**, inst**ant**, tempor**ary**, deliv**ery**, laborat**ory**, triumph**ant***.
- Look at other spelling features in the words and stress the pure vowel sound in ‹ery›, ‹ary›, ‹ory› and ‹ant› to help remember the spelling.

Spelling Point
- Introduce the spelling pattern ‹ist›, which often comes at the end of words and is used as a suffix to make nouns and some related adjectives. Nouns with the suffix ‹-ist› often indicate someone in a particular business or activity (e.g. *artist* or *tourist*) or someone who uses a particular thing, such as a *cyclist* or *guitarist*.
- Call out these nouns that indicate a particular profession or interest and see if the children can guess what the people they belong to do: *dentist, violinist, florist, scientist, novelist, canoeist*.
- Remind the children that not all ‹ist› words use the suffix: *exist* and *resist* are not nouns and simply happen to be spelt this way.

Spelling List
- Read the spelling words with the children, go over the meaning of any words they may not know, and ask them to find and highlight the ‹ist› spelling in each word.
- Point out the ‹s› saying /z/ in *resist*, the ‹ch› saying /k/ in *chemist*, the soft ‹c› in *cyclist* and *specialist*, the ‹y› spelling of /ie/ in *cyclist*, each ‹o› saying /oa/ in *soloist*, the silent ‹u› in *guitarist* (which is part of the silent letter digraph ‹gu›), the silent letter digraph ‹sc› in *scientist*, the ‹gu› saying /gw/ in *linguist* and the ‹ou› saying little /oo/ in *tourist*.
- It is a good idea to blend and sound out the spelling words quickly every day with the children, emphasising the pure sound of any schwas to help remember the spelling.

Spelling List
exist
resist
twist
insist
artist
consist
chemist
cyclist
florist
persist
soloist
specialist
guitarist
scientist
linguist
tourist
journalist
therapist

Activity Page
- The children find the spelling words in the word

search, looking for words going down as well as across. They then draw a picture to represent each of the people in the boxes, showing what they do.
- Finally, they parse the sentence, identify the subject (*scientist*) and then parse the verb (3rd person singular, present continuous). *His* is a possessive adjective describing who the experiment belongs to. All parts of the verb should be underlined in red.

The <u>scientist</u> <u>is persisting</u> <u>with</u> <u>his</u> <u>dangerous</u> <u>experiment</u>.

Dictation
- Provide a sheet of paper for each child and dictate the following sentences:

1. She insisted it was necessary to visit the florist.
2. The soloist we heard at the rehearsal was a pianist.
3. Miss Beech said, "The novelist wrote brilliantly."

Extension Activity
- Write these noun phrases on the board: *the smiling florist; green and purple thistles; two gnarled old trees; a long-haired guitarist*. The children draw a picture to illustrate each one.
- They then write down two noun phrases of their own and draw pictures for them.
- If there is time, the children could also see how many words they can make using the letters in *physiotherapist*.

Grammar: Phrases, Clauses and Sentences

Aim
- Refine the children's understanding of phrases and sentences by introducing the idea of clauses.
- A clause is a group of words that makes sense and has both a verb and a subject. When it can stand alone as a simple sentence, it is called an independent clause.

Introduction
- Revise sentences and phrases. Remind the children that all sentences must make sense, start with a capital letter, contain a verb and subject, and end with a full stop, question mark or exclamation mark. If the words make sense but there is no verb and subject, it is called a phrase.
- Also remind the children that the subject of a sentence 'does' the verb action and the object 'receives' the verb action.
- Write some examples on the board and ask the children to identify whether they are phrases or simple sentences: *in my swimming class* (phrase), *a moment in time* (phrase), *at the restaurant* (phrase), *I saw a boy in the distance* (sentence), *He lost his memory* (sentence), *I saw a different doctor at the hospital* (sentence).
- Remind the children that a phrase consisting of a noun and all the words that describe (or modify) it is called a noun phrase. Ask the class to suggest some nouns and turn them into noun phrases with the children.

Main Point
- Explain that as well as sentences and phrases, there are also groups of words called clauses.
- A clause is a group of words that contains a subject and verb and makes sense. This makes them sound like sentences and, indeed, some clauses can also be sentences.
- Write *He was tired so he went to bed* on the board. Remind the children about compound sentences, where two simple sentences are joined by one of the conjunctions *for, and, nor, but, or, yet* or *so* (known as co-ordinating conjunctions).
- Underline *He was tired* and *he went to bed*. Explain that although they can both stand alone as simple sentences, when they are part of a longer sentence they are called clauses.
- Now write *Because he was tired, he went to bed* on the board. Discuss the two clauses. The clause *he went to bed* can stand alone as a simple sentence.
- However, *Because he was tired* cannot as it is not a complete thought: although it has a subject and verb and makes sense, it leaves us to ask what happened *because he was tired*.

Phrases, Clauses and Sentences

REMEMBER A **phrase** is a group of words that makes sense but does not have a verb with a subject. A **clause** is a group of words that makes sense and has both a verb and a subject. An **independent clause** is a clause that can also stand alone as a simple sentence.

Look at each group of words below. If there is a verb, underline it in red and put a box with a small ‹s› in the corner around the subject; then circle the word 'clause'. If there is no verb and subject, circle 'phrase'.

we are going to the restaurant	phrase / clause
the old gnarled oak tree	phrase / clause
when she was young	phrase / clause
a large box of chocolates	phrase / clause
under the mistletoe	phrase / clause
they were digging up a fossil	phrase / clause
while we waited outside	phrase / clause
at the bottom of the box	phrase / clause
although she was tired	phrase / clause
he will write a sequel to the novel	phrase / clause
the blacksmith's anvil	phrase / clause
the lady with a hat	phrase / clause
as he ran around the corner	phrase / clause
inside the dark wardrobe	phrase / clause
the cook was adding some basil to the stew	phrase / clause

Look again at the clauses above and put a star next to those that could also be sentences; they are called independent clauses. Choose one and write it down as a sentence, giving it a capital letter and full stop.

61

- Tell the children that clauses that can stand alone as simple sentences are called independent clauses. Those that depend on some more information are called dependent or subordinate clauses.
- Later on, the children can learn that a sentence with an independent clause and a dependent clause is called a complex sentence.

Activity Page
- The children read each group of words and decide whether it is a phrase or a clause. If it is a clause, they underline the verb in red and draw a box around the subject, with a small ‹s› in the corner. If there is no verb and subject, it is a phrase. The children then put a star against the independent clauses (clause*, phrase, clause, phrase, phrase, clause*, clause, phrase, clause, clause*, phrase, phrase, clause, phrase, clause*).
- Finally, they choose an independent clause and write it as a sentence, adding a capital letter and full stop.

Extension Activity
- The children write the other independent clauses as sentences, adding a capital letter and full stop to each one.

Rounding Off
- Go over the activity page with the children, checking their answers.

Spelling: ‹pre-›

Spelling Test
- The children turn to the backs of their books and find the column labelled *Spelling Test 30*.
- In any order, call out the spelling words learnt last week. The children write the words on the lines.

Revision
- Revise prefixes, which are one or more syllables added at the beginning of a word to change or add meaning.
- Write these words on the board, identify the prefixes, and discuss how they modify the meaning: **un**happy (*not*), **de**scend (*down*), **dis**mount (*undo*), **mis**count (*wrongly*), **im**proper (*not*), **non**sense (*not*), **re**cycle (*again*).

Spelling Point
- Write *prefix* on the board and ask the children whether they know what the letters ‹pre› mean in words like *prepare*, *prevent* and *predict*. If you are prepared, you are ready for something before it happens; if you prevent something, you stop it before it happens; and if you predict something, you guess it will happen before it does.
- Explain that ‹pre-› is a prefix meaning *before*, so *prefix* means *fixed before*. That is why the letters in a prefix are added before the root word.
- Ask the children if they can think of any words beginning with the prefix ‹pre-›.

Spelling List
- Read the spelling words with the children, go over the meaning of any words they may not know, and ask them to find and highlight the ‹pre› spelling in each word.
- Point out any schwas, such as in *predecessor* and *previous*, the ‹are› spelling of /air/ in *prepare*, the ‹iew› saying /ue/ in *preview*, the ‹e_e› spelling of /ee/ in *precede*, the soft ‹c› in *precede*, *precedent*, *preference* and *predecessor*, the ‹ere› spelling of /air/ in *premiere*, the suffixes in *preced**ent**, *prehistoric*, *previously*, *preliminary* and *precautionary*, the ‹ture› in *premature*, the ‹ss› in *predecessor* and the ‹rr› in *prearrange*, the ‹s› saying /z/ and the silent ‹p› in *presumption*, and the ‹au› and ‹tion› in *precautionary*.
- It is a good idea to blend and sound out the spelling words quickly every day, emphasising the pure sound of any schwas to help remember the spelling.

prepare
prevent
prefix
prevail
preview
predict
precede
premiere
precedent
prehistoric
preference
premature
previously
predecessor
prearrange
preliminary
presumption
precautionary

Activity Page
- The children write a sentence for each of the listed spelling words.
- They then think of a word beginning with each prefix and write them underneath the fish heads.
- Finally, they parse the sentence, identify the subject (*delays*) and then parse the verb (3rd person plural, past continuous).

Delays were preventing the premiere of a controversial new play.

Dictation
- Dictate the following sentences:

1. They prepared to ascend the majestic mountain.
2. The cyclists had not predicted the abysmal weather.
3. Prehistoric creatures preceded our modern animals.

Extension Activity
- Write the following phrases and clauses on the board: *I prefer these accessories; because they were hungry; when the journalist called; many prehistoric dinosaurs; while he prepared dinner; in the scientist's laboratory; all the artist's sketches; a persistent cough; we finished the preparations.*
- The children decide whether each group of words is a phrase or a clause and put a star against the independent clauses (clause*, clause, clause, phrase, clause, phrase, phrase, phrase, clause*).

Grammar: Infinitives

Aim
- Reinforce the children's understanding of verbs and develop their ability to recognise the infinitive in a sentence.

Introduction
- Remind the children that sentences can be written in the first, second or third person, singular or plural, and must contain a verb.
- Verbs describe what is happening in the past, present or future and can be written in either the simple or continuous tenses.
- Call out some sentences and ask the children which tense each one is in: *I prepare dinner* (simple present); *I shall be preparing dinner* (future continuous); *I prepared dinner* (simple past); *He was walking the dog* (past continuous); *He will walk the dog* (simple future); *He is walking the dog* (present continuous).
- Conjugate a verb in the simple and continuous tenses with the children, doing the pronoun actions (see Personal Pronouns, page 9).

Main Point
- Explain that when we talk about a verb in general terms, we use the infinitive form.
- The infinitive, or name, of the verb usually has the word *to* in front of it, as in *to cook*, *to read*, *to sing*, and *to dive*.
- It is the simplest form of the verb and is what we would look up in the dictionary. As such, it does not have a tense or person; *to cook*, for example, does not tell us who is cooking or when there is cooking.
- Infinitives can be used in sentences, although they are never the main verb and do not have a subject.
- Write *Jim decides to stay at home* on the board and ask the children whether they can see an infinitive.
- Underline *to stay* in grey and ask them whether this is the main verb. (If it is it will have a subject.)
- Remind the children that the subject of a sentence does the verb action, but in this sentence nobody is *staying* yet. Ask them if there is another verb in the sentence and underline *decides* in red.
- Ask *Who or what decides?* to find the subject and draw a box with a small ‹s› in the corner around *Jim*.
- Write some more sentences with infinitives on the board and identify the infinitive, main verb and subject in each one.

Activity Page
- The children write inside the outlined word *Verbs*, using a red pencil. They then draw a picture in each flower to illustrate the infinitive.

- Next, they look at the pictures and write the infinitives underneath (*to cycle, to paint, to read, to eat, to dig, to write, to ski, to cook*).
- It does not matter if the verb that is chosen is different to the one given here, as long as it makes sense and is written correctly as an infinitive.
- Finally, the children identify the infinitive, main verb and subject in each sentence (*to eat, preferred, He^s; to cook, will be helping, I^s; to speak, demanded, She^s; to sing, yearned, student^s; to be, pretended, children^s; to see, hoped, tourist^s*).

Extension Activity
- Provide a sheet of paper for each child.
- Ask the children to think of some infinitives.
- Then, each child writes one of the infinitives at the top of their sheet of paper and draws a picture to illustrate it underneath.
- The pictures could be turned into a wall display, or made into a book for the children to use.

Rounding Off
- Go over the activity page with the children, checking their answers.

Spelling: ‹sub-›

Spelling Test
- The children turn to the backs of their books and find the column labelled *Spelling Test 31*.
- Call out the spelling words learnt last week.

Revision
- Revise prefixes, which are one or more syllables added at the beginning of a word to change or add meaning.
- Write these words on the board, identify the prefixes, and discuss how they modify the meaning: *prefix* (before), *unkind* (not), *decaffeinated* (remove), *disappear* (undo), *impossible* (not), *return* (again), *misplace* (wrongly).

Spelling Point
- Write *submerge*, *subheading* and *sub-zero* on the board and ask the children whether they know what the letters ‹sub› mean. If something is submerged, it goes under the water; a subheading is one that goes below the main heading; and if there are sub-zero temperatures, the temperature is below zero.
- Explain that ‹sub-› is a prefix meaning *below* or *under*. Ask the children if they can think of any words beginning with the prefix ‹sub-›.

Spelling List
- Read the spelling words with the children, go over the meaning of any words they may not know, and ask them to find and highlight the ‹sub› spelling in each word.
- Point out any schwas, such as in *subterranean* and *subconscious*, the ‹i_e› saying /ie/ in *subside* and *subdivide*, the ‹ay› spelling on the end of *subway*, how a 'magic' vowel can change a short stressed vowel in the previous syllable into the long vowel sound, as in *subtitle*, *sub-zero*, *subordinate* and *subterranean*, but not in *submission* and *submissive*, where the double consonant blocks the influence of the schwa (the first ‹e› in *subterranean* is similarly protected).
- Point out the ‹sion› in *submission*, the soft ‹g› in *submerge*, the ‹le› in *subtitle* and *submersible*, the hyphen separating the suffix and root word in *sub-zero*, the ‹o› saying /oa/ at the end of *sub-zero*, the ‹ea› saying /e/ in *subheading*, the ‹i_e› saying /ee/ in *submarine*, the ‹ive› saying /iv/ in *submissive* and the silent letter digraph ‹sc› in *subconscious*.

submit
subdue
subplot
subside
subvert
subway
subdivide
submission
submerge
subtitle
sub-zero
submersible
subheading
subordinate
submarine
submissive
subconscious
subterranean

Activity Page
- The children unscramble the letters in the submarines and add them to ‹sub› to make words from the spelling list (*subway, subdue, submit, subtitle, submarine, subplot, subconscious, subheading, submerge, subvert, subdivide, subterranean, subside*).
- They look up the word *subterranean* in the dictionary and see how many other words they can make using its letters. Finally, they parse the sentence, identify the subject (*earth*) and then parse the verb (3rd person singular, present continuous). The earth from the subsidence is blocking the subterranean tunnels.

Dictation
- Dictate the following sentences:

1. Giant crystals exist in the subterranean cavern.
2. Tourists visited the wreck in a small submersible.
3. "The submarines were fantastic!" exclaimed Dad.

Extension Activity
- Write these words on the board: *careless, inactive, depart, unsuccessful, disappear, unknowable, misbehave, impatiently*. The children divide each word into its root and prefix and/or suffix (*care/less, in/active, de/part, un/success/ful, dis/appear, un/know/able, mis/behave, im/patient/ly*).

Grammar: Onomatopoeia

Aim
• Introduce the children to the idea of onomatopoeia, where the sound of a word relates to what it is describing. Develop their ability to make their writing more interesting and expressive.

Introduction
• The word *onomatopoeia* comes from the Greek words for *to make* and *name*, meaning *the name I make*. Onomatopoeic words are words that describe a sound by imitating that sound.
• One common group of onomatopoeic words is animal noises; *oink, baa, meow* and *cock-a-doodle-do* are just a few of the many words used to describe the different sounds animals make.
• Other groups include words related to the voice (*giggle, gurgle, grunt, growl*), to water (*trickle, plop, splash, drip*), to things moving through the air (*whoosh, swish, whizz, flutter*) and to things colliding (*thud, clang, smash, slap*).

Main Point
• Ask the children how an explosion in a comic book might be shown. As well as a picture, for example, the words *bang* or *boom* might appear like this. If possible, show the children some pictures from comic books and look at the different words used, such as *kaboom, pow, whack* and *wham*.
• Ask some of the children to say these words with expression, and discuss how the words themselves sound like the actions they are describing.
• Explain that when we use words like this in our writing, it is called onomatopoeia.
• Point out that not all onomatopoeic words describe things colliding: *buzz* sounds like the noise a bee makes and *boing* sounds like a spring jumping up.
• Give some more examples of onomatopoeic words and ask the children to suggest what they might be describing: *pop* (a balloon bursting), *crunch* (a rabbit eating a carrot), *atishoo* (someone sneezing), *cuckoo* (the call of a cuckoo or a cuckoo clock), *gurgle* (water going down the drain), *purr* (a happy cat) and *splash* (something falling into water).
• Ask the children if they can think of other words like this and discuss them with the class.
• Explain that onomatopoeia is often used in songs and poetry to make the writing more interesting and expressive. Use some examples from poems the children will know or have studied recently in class.

Activity Page
• The children trace over the onomatopoeic words at the top of the sheet. They then think of an appropriate word to describe the noise each animal makes (e.g. *roar, tweet, howl, croak, quack*) and to describe the sound made in each picture underneath (e.g. *clap, crackle, fizz*). It does not matter if the words that are chosen are different to the ones given here, as long as they make sense.
• Next, the children draw a picture to illustrate each of the onomatopoeic words below: for example, a plate breaking (*smash*), something frying in a pan (*sizzle*) and a mouse (*squeak*). Finally they match the noun phrases and onomatopoeic words at the bottom of the sheet (*purr, screech, tinkle, slurp, honk, thud*).

Extension Activity
• The children think of more onomatopoeic words that describe animal noises. They draw a picture of each animal with a speech bubble around the words.
• They could then use the words to write an 'animal chatter' poem or song. Examples include: *cuckoo, meow, oink, baa, buzz, cluck, hiss, honk, roar, tweet, growl, howl, croak, ribbit, quack, squeak, purr, screech, woof, squawk, chirp, bark, whine, cheep, twitter, moo, neigh*.

Rounding Off
• Go over the children's work, checking their answers.

95

Spelling: ‹anti-›

Spelling Test
- The children turn to the backs of their books and find the column labelled *Spelling Test 32*.
- Call out the spelling words learnt last week.

Revision
- Revise prefixes, which are one or more syllables added at the beginning of a word to change or add meaning.
- Write these words on the board, identify the prefixes, and discuss how they modify the meaning: **pre**suppose (*before*), **sub**merge (*under*), **de**frost (*remove*), **mis**behave (*wrongly*), **semi**circle (*half*), **im**mobile (*not*), **re**do (*again*).

Spelling Point
- Write *anti-war*, *anti-hero* and *antibacterial* on the board and ask the children whether they know what the letters ‹anti› mean. An anti-war protester is someone who is against war; the anti-hero in a story is the opposite of a hero; and if something is antibacterial, it acts against bacteria.
- Explain that ‹anti-› is a prefix meaning *opposed*, as in *against*, *opposite to* or *preventing*.
- Ask the children if they can think of any words beginning with the prefix ‹anti-›.

Spelling List
- Read the spelling words with the children and ask them to highlight the ‹anti› spelling in each word.
- Point out any schwas, such as in *antipathy* and *antithesis*, the ‹or› saying /ar/ after ‹w› in *anti-war*, the hyphen separating the suffix and root word in *anti-war*, *anti-hero*, *anti-aircraft*, *anti-dandruff* and *anti-perspirant*, the ‹y› saying /ee/ on the end of *antibody* and *antipathy,* and the ‹o_e› saying /oa/ in *antidote* and *anticyclone*.
- Also point out the suffixes in *antisep**tic**, antibiot**ic**, antisoc**ial**, antibacter**ial**, antioxid**ant*** and *anti-perspir**ant***, how a 'magic' vowel can change a short stressed vowel in the previous syllable into the long vowel sound, as in *antisocial*, *anticlimax* and *antibiotic*, but not in *antimatter*, where the double consonant blocks the influence of the schwa.
- Point out the ‹ze› saying /z/ in *antifreeze*, the soft ‹c› in *anticyclone*, the ‹y› saying /ie/ in *anticyclone*, the ‹ff› at the end of *anti-dandruff*, the ‹x› in *antioxidant* and the ‹ir› spelling in *anti-perspirant*.

anti-war
anti-hero
antibody
antidote
antiseptic
antimatter
antifreeze
antisocial
antipathy
anticlimax
anticyclone
anti-aircraft
anti-dandruff
antibiotic
antithesis
antioxidant
antibacterial
anti-perspirant

Activity Page
- The children write words in the fish, putting the prefix (*anti*) in the head and the root in the body.
- They then write an onomatopoeic word for each picture (possible answers: *atishoo, boom, splash*).
- Next, they add punctuation to the sentences (1. *I bought anti-perspirant, toothpaste, antibacterial soap, anti-dandruff shampoo and a bottle of antiseptic.* 2. *"What an anticlimax!" exclaimed Meena.* 3. *The captain asked, "Are the submarine crew on deck?"*).
- Finally, they parse the sentence, identify the subject (*doctor*) and then parse the verb (3rd person singular, simple present). *Quickly* is an adverb made by adding ‹-ly› to the adjective *quick*. *Snake's* is a possessive noun, which acts as an adjective.

The <u>doctor</u> <u>quickly</u> <u>gives</u> <u>him</u> the <u>antidote</u> <u>for</u> the <u>snake's</u> <u>venom</u>.

Dictation
- Dictate the following sentences:

1. "I bought some anti-dandruff shampoo," said Jill.
2. Antifreeze is necessary in sub-zero temperatures.
3. Antibodies in his blood killed the harmful bacteria.

Extension Activity
- Write these onomatopoeic words on the board: *flutter, drip, gurgle, slurp, honk, snap.*
- The children draw a picture for each word.

Grammar: Hyphens

Aim
- Refine the children's knowledge of punctuation and develop their ability to use a hyphen.

Introduction
- Remind the class that punctuation is important because it helps us make sense of the words we use.
- Ask the children what punctuation they know (full stops, question marks, exclamation marks, speech marks, commas and apostrophes) and discuss when they might use them.
- Point out that speech marks and apostrophes appear above the line and write them on the board.
- Now remind the children that they have also come across another type of punctuation in their recent spelling lessons. Write *sub-zero*, *anti-dandruff* and *anti-hero* on the board and tell them that the small line separating the prefix and root word is called a hyphen. Point out that the hyphen also sits above the line, but not as far up as the apostrophe or speech marks.

Main Point
- Explain that as well as linking a prefix and root word, a hyphen is often used to link whole words together to make compound words. The hyphen shows that each word is related to the other and also makes some compound words easier to read, as in *sister-in-law*.
- However, whether or not a compound word or a word with a prefix needs a hyphen can change over time or depend on which dictionary you refer to. For example, as *e-mail* (short for *electronic mail*) grew in popularity it became *email*. Similarly, *co-operate* can be written with or without the hyphen (using the hyphen makes the prefix ‹co-› more obvious).
- A good rule of thumb is to use a hyphen when it makes things clearer.
- To demonstrate how hyphens' usage can affect meaning, write two sentences on the board: *The 12-year-old snakes* and *The 12 year-old snakes*. Ask the children how the different uses of the hyphen change the meaning: the first describes an unspecified number of snakes that are twelve years old and the second describes twelve snakes that are a year old. Until the children know how to use hyphenated words, it is best to look them up in a dictionary.
- There are, however, some circumstances in which a hyphen is nearly always used.
- Call out some numbers between 21 and 99 and write them on the board as words, revising the spelling of any the children are not sure of. When writing a compound number, such as *twenty-one*, add the hyphen and explain that it is used to show

that the number is 21 and not the two numbers, twenty and one.
- The hyphen is also used when the first word in a compound word is a capital letter, as in *X-ray* and *T-shirt*.
- Other common uses of the hyphen include joining fractions (*three-quarters, two-thirds*) and compound adjectives that come before the nouns they are describing, as in *the friendly-looking boy*, but the children can learn about these later. For now it is enough that they understand what a hyphen is and how it can be used to make meaning clearer.

Activity Page
- The children trace over the dotted words. They then write the numbers as words, separated with a hyphen (*forty-two, fifty-eight, twenty-one, seventy-five, thirty-six, ninety-three*). Next they use *X-ray*, *U-turn* and *T-shirt* in a sentence, looking up the words in a dictionary if necessary.
- Finally, they write the correct hyphenated word to complete each sentence (*brother-in-law, self-portrait, left-handed, check-in, life-size, break-in*).

Extension Activity
- The children turn the dotted noun phrases (*a far-flung destination, an emerald-green lizard, a long-tailed kite, a one-eyed ogre*) into sentences, perhaps trying to use all four in a short story.

Spelling: ‹trans-›

Spelling Test
- The children turn to the backs of their books and find the column labelled *Spelling Test 33*.
- Call out the spelling words learnt last week.

Revision
- Revise prefixes, which are one or more syllables added at the beginning of a word to change or add meaning.
- Write these words on the board, identify the prefixes, and discuss how they modify the meaning: **pre**view (*before*), **sub**way (*under*), **anti**social (*opposite*), **dis**agree (*undo*), **re**fund (*again*), **im**perfect (*not*), **ex**-student (*former*). Sometimes there is a hyphen between the prefix and the root word.

Spelling Point
- Write *transport*, *transparent* and *transform* on the board and ask the children whether they know what the letters ‹trans› mean. If you transport something by plane, you fly it from one place across to another; if something is transparent, it means you can see through it; and if something is transformed, it is completely changed.
- Explain that ‹trans-› is a prefix meaning *across*, *through* or *changed*.
- Ask the children if they can think of any words beginning with the prefix ‹trans-›.

Spelling List
- Read the spelling words with the children and ask them to find and highlight the ‹trans› spelling in each word.
- Point out any schwas, such as in *transmitter* and *transferable*, how the ‹s› in the prefix sometimes says /z/, as in *transit*, how a 'magic' vowel can change a short stressed vowel in the previous syllable into the long vowel sound, as in *translate*, *transpose*, *transfusion*, *translation* and *transformation*, but not in *transmitter*, where the double consonant blocks the influence of the schwa.
- Point out the ‹se› saying /s/ on the end of *transverse*, the silent letter digraph ‹sc› in *transcend*, the ‹tion› saying /shun/ in *transaction*, *translation* and *transformation*, the suffixes in *transitory*, *transparent* and *transferable*, and the ‹sion› saying /zhun/ in *transfusion*.

transport
transfer
transmit
transept
transit
translate
transpose
transverse
transmitter
transcend
transplant
transaction
transitory
transfusion
transparent
translation
transferable
transformation

Activity Page
- The children fill in the missing letters (*transfer, transplant, transport, transcend, transmitter, transit, transferable, transformation, transept, transverse, translate, transpose, transmit, transitory*). Then, they look at the pictures and write the infinitives underneath (*to eat, to read, to hike, to bounce*). It does not matter if the verb that is chosen is different to the one given here, as long as it makes sense and is written correctly as an infinitive.
- Finally, the children parse the sentence, identify the subject (*museum*) and then parse the verb (3rd person singular, future continuous). *Transport* is a noun acting as an adjective and *dramatic* is an adjective with the ‹-ic› suffix.

The transport museum will be undergoing a dramatic transformation.

Dictation
- Dictate the following sentences:

1. He twisted the dial on the radio transmitter.
2. "A linguist will translate for me," said the journalist.
3. He was transferred to another ward in the hospital.

Extension Activity
- The children write down as many forms of transport as they can and think about where each one might go.

Grammar: Antonyms and Synonyms

Aim
- Reinforce the children's understanding of antonyms and synonyms and develop their ability to use a wider variety of words in their writing.

Introduction
- Briefly revise how to use dictionaries and thesauruses, and remind the children that they can use a thesaurus to find synonyms and antonyms for a particular word.
- Make sure the children know the difference between synonyms and antonyms. Synonyms are words that have the same or similar meaning to the word being looked up, whereas antonyms (opposites), are words with the opposite meaning.
- Remind the children that many prefixes and some suffixes can be used to make antonyms.
- Call out some words and ask the class to suggest an antonym for each one: *sad* (*happy*), *dark* (*light*), *up* (*down*), *good* (*bad*), *untidy* (*tidy*), *powerful* (*powerless*).
- Then write some word pairs on the board and ask whether they are antonyms or synonyms: *achieve, succeed* (synonyms), *entrance, exit* (antonyms), *maximum, minimum* (antonyms), *avoid, miss* (synonyms).

Main Point
- Remind the children that using a variety of words can help to make their writing more interesting and avoid overusing certain words. However, it is important to remember that words can have more than one meaning, so the children must check that the synonym they choose does not change the meaning of their sentence significantly.
- Write *The acrobats were amazing* on the board. Ask the children to think of synonyms for *amazing* (e.g. *wonderful, remarkable, brilliant, incredible, awesome*) and write them on the board in a word web.
- Read the sentence again with the class, each time substituting *amazing* with a different synonym. Check that all the synonyms have the same general meaning.
- Now ask the children for some antonyms for *amazing* (e.g. *awful, dreadful, hopeless, terrible, appalling*).
- Write the suggestions under the web, putting a box around them to keep them separate.

Activity Page
- The children read each set of words and cross out any that are not synonyms of the word in the

spider's web (cross out: *feathery, dense, maximum, difficult, pinched, familiar*).
- Then they write an antonym for each word in the mirrors (possible answers: *rough, true, unusual, similar, straight, confident*). It does not matter if the children use different words to the ones here, as long as they make sense.
- Finally, they think of two synonyms and an antonym for each word at the bottom of the sheet and write them in the word webs (possible answers: *interesting: exciting, gripping, boring; abominable: awful, dreadful, wonderful; immense: huge, vast, tiny; comfortable: cosy, relaxed, uneasy; handsome: attractive, charming, ugly; bizarre: strange, odd, normal*). The children may want to use a thesaurus to help them think of suitable words, or to check that they are correct.

Extension Activity
- The children choose some words from the worksheet and write a sentence for each one. Then they rewrite the sentences, using a suitable antonym.

Rounding Off
- Go over the activity page with the children, checking their answers. If they have done the extension activity, ask some of the children to read out their sentences.

99

Spelling: ‹inter-›

Spelling Test
- The children turn to the backs of their books and find the column labelled *Spelling Test 34*.
- In any order, call out the spelling words learnt last week. The children write the words on the lines.

Revision
- Revise prefixes, which are one or more syllables added at the beginning of a word to change or add meaning.
- Write these words on the board, identify the prefixes, and discuss how they modify the meaning: **pre**caution (*before*), **sub**-zero (*under*), **anti**freeze (*opposite*), **trans**form (*change*), **un**pleasant (*not*), **mid**day (*middle*), **non**-smoker (*not*). Sometimes there is a hyphen between the prefix and the root word.

Spelling Point
- Write *interval*, *interview* and *international* on the board and ask the children whether they know what the letters ‹inter› mean. If a play has an interval, there is a break between the start and finish; an interview is a meeting between two (or more) people to find out information; and an international law is one that is recognised among many nations.
- Explain that ‹inter-› is a prefix meaning *between* or *among*. Ask the children if they can think of any words beginning with the prefix ‹inter-›.

Spelling List
- Read the spelling words with the children, go over the meaning of any words they may not know, and ask them to find and highlight the ‹inter› spelling in each word.
- Point out any schwas, such as in *interval* and *interpreter* and how a 'magic' vowel can change a short stressed vowel in the previous syllable into the long vowel sound, as in *interlude*, *intervene*, and *interloper*, but not in *intermittent*, where the double consonant blocks the influence of the schwa.
- Point out the ‹ck› in *interlock*, the ‹ive› saying /ve/ on the end of *interactive*, the ‹iew› saying /ue/ in *interview*, the ‹a› saying /ai/ in *interchange*, the ‹ere› saying /ear/ in *interfere*, the soft ‹c› in *intercept*, the ‹ea› saying /ee/ and ‹ve› saying /v/ in *interweave*, and the suffixes in *intermitt**ent*** and *internation**al***.
- Also point out the ‹tion› in *international*, and how the first ‹a› says /ai/ in *nation* but /a/ in *national*.

interact
interval
intersect
internet
interlock
interlude
interactive
interview
interject
intervene
interpreter
interchange
interloper
interfere
intercept
interweave
intermittent
international

Activity Page
- The children put the spelling words in alphabetical order (*interact, interactive, intercept, interchange, interfere, interject, interlock, interloper, interlude, intermittent, international, internet, interpreter, intersect, interval, intervene, interview, interweave*).
- Next, they write a question using a spelling word, which they then rewrite as a statement, using the correct punctuation.
- Finally, they parse the sentence, identify the subject (*They*) and then parse the verb (3rd person plural, simple past). *Spanish* is a proper adjective and *Wednesday* is a proper noun and both need a capital letter.

They interviewed a new Spanish interpreter on Wednesday.

Dictation
- Dictate the following sentences:

1. There are many interactive games on the internet.
2. "The rain will be intermittent," said the weatherman.
3. "Will the play have an interval?" asked the parents.

Extension Activity
- Write these words on the board: *angry, sleepy, under, quick, nasty, succeed, finish, afraid, quiet*.
- The children think of two synonyms and an antonym for each word.

Grammar: More Homophone Mix-Ups (2)

Aim
- Reinforce the children's understanding of homophones and develop their ability to choose between similar-sounding words in their writing.

Introduction
- Ask the children to call out some of the homophones that they have learnt so far. The main ones are: *our* and *are*; *their*, *there* and *they're*; *your* and *you're*; *its* and *it's*; *to*, *two* and *too*; and *where*, *wear* and *were*. Make sure the children know which spellings take which meanings.
- *Our* is more properly pronounced /ou-r/ but in practice it is often pronounced /ar/ and can be confused with *are*.
- *Were* is not strictly a homophone of *where*, but their spellings are often confused so it helps to look at them together.
- Point out that some of these words are parts of the verb *to be* (*are*, *were*) and some are possessive adjectives (*our*, *your*, *their*, *its*), while others are contractions (*they're*, *you're*, *it's*).
- Children often find *its* and *it's* particularly difficult because apostrophe ‹s› can also be used to show possession; however, it is only used in this way to make possessive nouns and not possessive adjectives, and *its* is a possessive adjective.
- Remind the children that it is important to use the correct spelling when writing homophones, otherwise their writing will not make sense.

Main Point
- Ask the children if they can think of any other homophones and write them on the board. The children may remember the examples from pages 4, 40 and 57 of the *Pupil Book*, and they may know some others.
- Write some of the homophones from the bottom of the activity page on the board, discussing their spelling and meanings: *see, sea; ewe, you, yew; would, wood; daze, days; brake, break; clause, claws; right, write; for, four; ate, eight; pair, pear; be, bee.*
- If the children are unsure of the meaning of any of the homophones, ask them to look up the words in the dictionary. See who can find the definitions first.
- Remind the children that they need to stop and think before writing a homophone, decide which meaning is needed, and think how the word with that meaning is spelt.
- Ask the children to think of sentences for some of the homophones and discuss which spellings they would use.

Activity Page
- The children read the sentences, decide which word(s) are needed to complete each one and write them in (*your; you're; Where; wear; were; two, to, too; there; their; they're; its; It's*).
- They then write a homophone for each of the words at the bottom of the sheet (*see, sea; ewe, you* or *yew; would, wood; daze, days; brake, break; clause, claws; right, write; for, four; ate, eight; pair, pear*).

Extension Activity
- The children write sentences using some of the homophones from the bottom of the activity page.
- They could work in pairs, taking it in turns to dictate a sentence, and then decide together whether the correct spelling has been used.

Rounding Off
- Go over the activity page with the children, checking their answers. If they have done the extension activity, ask some of the children to read out their sentences.

Spelling: ‹tele-›

Spelling Test
- The children turn to the backs of their books and find the column labelled *Spelling Test 35*.
- In any order, call out the spelling words learnt last week. The children write the words on the lines.

Revision
- Revise prefixes, which are one or more syllables added at the beginning of a word to change or add meaning.
- Write these words on the board, identify the prefixes, and discuss how they modify the meaning: **pre**arrange (*before*), **sub**marine (*under*), **anti**-dandruff (*against*), **trans**atlantic (*across*), **inter**national (*between*), **ex**hale (*out*), **non**stop (*not*).
- Sometimes there is a hyphen between the prefix and the root word.

Spelling Point
- Write *telescope*, *telephone* and *television* on the board and ask the children whether they know what the letters ‹tele› mean. A telescope allows you to see clearly things that are far away; you can speak to someone on a telephone, even if they are in another country; and you watch things on a television that are happening somewhere else.
- Explain that ‹tele-› is a prefix meaning *far off* or *at a distance*. Ask the children if they can think of any words beginning with the prefix ‹tele-›.

Spelling List
- Read the spelling words with the children, go over the meaning of any words they may not know, and ask them to find and highlight the ‹tele› spelling in each word.
- Point out any schwas, such as in *tel**e**gram* and *tel**e**pathy* and how a 'magic' vowel can change a short stressed vowel in the previous syllable into the long vowel sound, as in *telesc**o**pe*, *teleph**o**ne*, *teleph**o**to*, *telev**i**se*, *telekin**e**sis* and *telecomm**u**ting*.
- Point out the ‹x› in *telex*, the suffixes in *telepath**ic***, *telescop**ic***, *telecommut**ing*** and *telemarket**ing***, the ‹ph› saying /f/ in *telegraph*, *telephone* and *telephoto*, the ‹o› saying /oa/ at the end of *telephoto*, the ‹s› saying /z/ in *televise*, the ‹y› saying /ee/ on the end of *telepathy*, the ‹sion› saying /zhun/ in *television*, the ‹k› in *telekinesis* and *telemarketing*, and the soft ‹c› in *teleconference*.

telex
telecast
telethon
telegram
teleport
telescope
telepathic
telegraph
telephone
telephoto
televise
telepathy
telescopic
television
telekinesis
teleconference
telecommuting
telemarketing

Activity Page
- The children put some of the spelling words into the prefix fish, writing the prefix (*tele*) in the head and the root in the body.
- They then check the meaning of the word *telecommunications* in the dictionary and see how many other words they can make using its letters.
- Finally, they parse the sentence, identify the subject (*I*) and then parse the verb (1st person singular, simple future). *Fantastic* is an adjective with the ‹-ic› suffix and should be underlined in blue. All parts of the verb should be underlined in red.

I will tell you about the fantastic telescope over the telephone.

Dictation
- Dictate the following sentences:

1. Telegrams were used to report important events.
2. "I found an old telephone in the shed," said Sam.
3. She bought a telephoto lens for her new camera.

Extension Activity
- Write these pairs of homophones on the board: *boulder* and *bolder*; *heirless* and *airless*; *assistants* and *assistance*; *groan* and *grown*; *waste* and *waist*.
- The children write a sentence for each homophone, using the correct meaning and spelling. They can use a dictionary to look up unfamiliar words.

Grammar: Changing Verb Tenses (2)

Aim
- Reinforce the children's knowledge of the simple and continuous tenses and develop their ability to rewrite a sentence in another tense.

Introduction
- Write *to look* on the board. Ask the children what this form of the verb is called (the infinitive).
- Then ask them who is looking and when: is it in the first, second or third person, is it singular or plural, and is it in the past, present or future?
- Remind the children that the infinitive does not give us this information, as it does not have a person or tense. It is the simplest form of the verb; we use it to talk about the verb in general terms or to look it up in a dictionary.
- Remind the children that infinitives are also used in sentences, although they are never the main verb and do not have a subject.

Main Point
- Draw a simple grid of six boxes on the board, each box large enough to write a simple sentence in.
- Ask the children to call out the names of the tenses they know and write them in the boxes.

simple past	simple present	simple future
past continuous	present continuous	future continuous

- Then ask the children to say a sentence in the simple present tense, such as *I ride my bike; He dances to the music;* or *They walk home from school.*
- Choose one of the sentences and write it in the *simple present* box or tent. Underline the verb and ask the class to rewrite it in one of the other tenses, or to suggest a new sentence for the next tense.
- Discuss how each tense is formed (see Verbs, pages 9 to 11), sometimes adding a suffix like ‹-ed› or ‹-ing›, sometimes by using an auxiliary like *shall* or *will*, and sometimes by adding both.
- Remind the children that when ‹-ing› is added to the verb it is called the present participle and that this form of the verb, along with the auxiliary verb *to be*, is used to make the continuous tenses. Also remind the children of the spelling rules for adding ‹-ed› and ‹-ing›, which depend on how the root verb is spelt:
- If the root verb ends in a consonant immediately after a short, stressed vowel sound, double the final consonant before adding the suffix, as in *stopped* and *hugging*.
- If the root verb ends in a consonant which is not immediately after a short vowel sound, simply add the suffix, as in *parted* and *parting*.
- If the root verb ends in ‹e›, remove it before adding the suffix, as in *loved* and *loving*. The only exception is when adding ‹-ing› to a root verb ending in ‹ie›: the ‹ie› is replaced by ‹-y› before the suffix is added, to avoid having two ‹i›s next to each other. That is why the present participle of *to lie* is *lying*, but the simple past is *lied*.
- If the root verb ends in ‹ay›, ‹ey› or ‹oy›, simply add the suffix, as in *stayed* and *staying*.
- If the root verb ends in a consonant followed by ‹y›, as in *tidy*, 'shy ‹i›' replaces the ‹y› in *tidied* because ‹i› is no longer at the end of the word, but not in *tidying* as it would look odd having two ‹i›s next to each other.

Activity Page
- The children write one or more sentences for each tense or rewrite the same sentence(s) each time. Write some verbs on the board for the children to use in their sentences (e.g. *to clap, to jump, to stay, to climb, to fry, to collect, to turn, to play, to bake, to dig, to walk, to sing, to run, to cook, to dance, to explore, to sniff, to sail, to fly, to swim, to read*).

Extension Activity
- The children work in pairs, identifying the tenses in each other's sentences. They then check whether they both agree.

Changing Verb Tenses — Verbs

Think of a verb and put it into a simple sentence, using one of the tenses below. Then rewrite the sentence in the other tenses, and add them to the correct tense tents. Alternatively, write a different sentence for each tense.

Simple Past · Past Continuous · Simple Present · Present Continuous · Simple Future · Future Continuous

73

The Grammar 5 Handbook

The teaching in *The Grammar 5 Handbook* follows on from that in the *Grammar 4 Pupil and Teacher's Books*. Throughout the course of this handbook, the children's understanding of language is further refined.

The children learn new elements of grammar, such as the past participle, transitive and intransitive verbs, phrasal verbs, prepositional phrases, the perfect tenses, and homographs, homonyms and heteronyms. They build upon their knowledge of sentence structure by learning about sentence walls, a simplified form of sentence digramming. The children also extend their understanding of adverbs; they learn that, in addition to verbs, adverbs can modify other adverbs and adjectives, and that adverbs can indicate manner, degree, place, time and frequency. They also learn how to write a list using a colon and bullet points.

In spelling, the children learn new spelling patterns like the prefixes ‹multi-›, ‹auto-›, ‹mega-› and ‹micro-›, and the suffixes ‹-ology›, ‹-ment›, ‹-ship› and ‹-ward›. The main focus of the spelling lessons in the *Grammar 5 Handbook* is on word families: words that share a common root and words with common prefixes and suffixes. Now that the children are older, there are two spelling activity sheets per lesson.

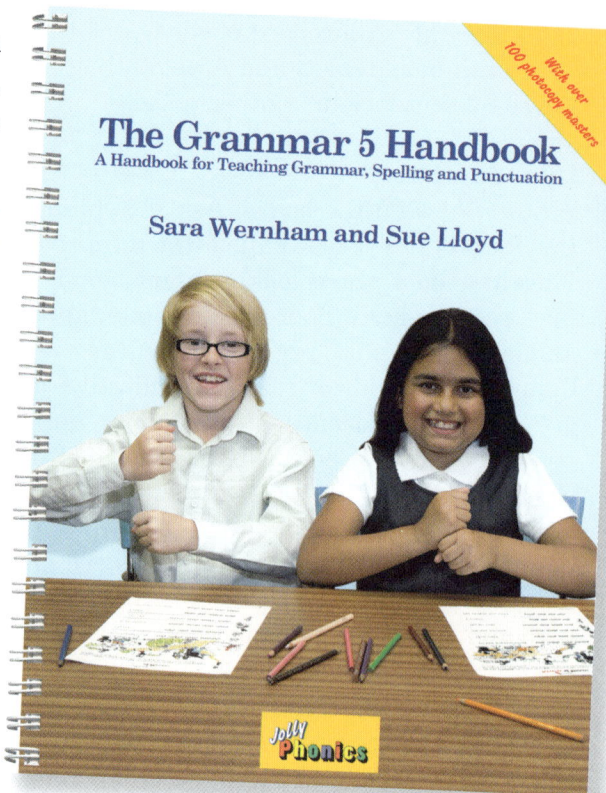